T0361550

THE BLACK PRACTICE OF DISBELIEF

THE **BLACK** **PRACTICE** OF **DISBELIEF**

**AN INTRODUCTION TO THE PRINCIPLES,
HISTORY, AND COMMUNITIES
OF BLACK NONBELIEVERS**

▲ ▲ ▲ ▲ ▲ ▲ ▲ ▲ ▲ ▲

ANTHONY B. PINN

BEACON PRESS, BOSTON

Beacon Press
Boston, Massachusetts
www.beacon.org

Beacon Press books
are published under the auspices of
the Unitarian Universalist Association of Congregations.

© 2024 by Anthony B. Pinn

All rights reserved
Printed in the United States of America

27 26 25 24   8 7 6 5 4 3 2 1

This book is printed on acid-free paper that meets the uncoated paper
ANSI/NISO specifications for permanence as revised in 1992.

Text design and composition by Kim Arney

Library of Congress Cataloging-in-Publication Data
is available for this title.
ISBN: 978-0-8070-4522-0; e-book: 978-0-8070-4523-7;
audiobook: 978-0-8070-3517-7

CONTENTS

INTRODUCTION

▲ ▲ ▲ ▲ ▲ ▲ ▲ ▲ ▲ ▲

I have grown to like "nontheist" as a broad-spectrum term that carries less baggage than more commonly used words such as "atheist" or "agnostic."

—CANDACE GORHAM

To do good is my religion.

—THOMAS PAINE

According to popular imagination in the United States, to be a Black American is to be a Black Christian. This connection is made, typically without any call for justification. It is grounded in a common narration of Black life that views its guiding concerns and questions as revolving around issues of transformation and revelation best discussed using the theological grammar and vocabulary of the dominant religious orientation of the United States: Christianity. Of course, there is something to this association, in that the vast majority of Black Americans claim some affiliation with Christianity—particularly one of the predominantly Black denominations. Yet this link has never captured the thinking, motivations, and orientation of all Black Americans. In fact, in recent years, a population of Black Americans who claim no connection to Christianity in general, or the Black Church in particular, has grown.

THE CHALLENGE OF CATEGORIES

As will become clear over the course of this book, there are a variety of names by which Black nontheists call themselves—for instance, atheists, skeptic, freethinker, or humanist. And while I wouldn't make the argument that they are synonymous, I would say that they point to overlapping concerns and claims that make the terminology used to describe this population somewhat flexible. One gets a sense of this in the following statement made by journalist Alejandra Molina: "Black nonbelievers . . . have for years been working to redefine what it means to be atheist, a word too often linked to white spaces mostly concerned with creationism and the separation of church and state. Many Black nonbelievers identify as humanist and challenge Christianity for being linked to racism, capitalism and sexism."[1] Shared social concerns provide something of a nexus that serves to "soften" the distinction of titles.

There are layers to this identity—complexities that too often are ignored. I believe this is what author and activist Sikivu Hutchinson is getting at when she writes that Black nontheists are typically truncated and reduced to one dimension of their identity that involves disbelief in God, and so "rejecting religion becomes an end in and of itself, and not merely symbolic of a more politicized belief system based on social justice, ethics, black liberation, black feminism and serving black communities within the context of heightened anti-Black state violence, segregation and misogynoir."[2] Again, this isn't to render these categories (e.g., humanist, atheist, skeptic) identical. It is to point out a fluid application that doesn't demand hard and fixed distinction, but instead sees each label addressing a particular dimension of a complex sense of self. I'll use a personal example: I understand myself to be a humanist, but there are conversations and times during which it is more productive to highlight a particular element of that identity. Therefore, I might call myself an atheist or a freethinker, depending on what is needed in a given context to best express what I understand as my commitments and aims. I would say I'm not alone in applying this strategy—in other words, there isn't necessarily a conflict in using a variety of description to captures one's nontheism. Keep in mind this claim when hearing Asher_Jak's self-identification: "I am an atheist. I'm also a skeptic. My atheism and skepticism are key parts in maintaining peace of mind, feeling in control of my life, and sometimes even healing."[3] Or think of the blending of terms in this statement by Ken Granderson: "For those not familiar with the word, a Humanist is basically an atheist who takes strong moral stances on things, or for whom morality is a clear and present factor in the thoughts and actions in their daily lives."[4] In all of these instances, there is a concern with behavior and beliefs beyond theistic assumptions.

For the purposes of this slim volume, I want to overturn the assumption that only Black theism in its various forms offers life orientation. By doing this, I move to the center of Black religious life a tradition that is typically misunderstood and marginalized. I present Black humanism in a new way, one that highlights its communal dimensions, its meaning-making rituals, and its belief structures. One gets a sense of this thinking with Sikivu Hutchinson, who explains her life and philosophical orientation, having been raised in a secular home, over against the theism encountered during a year attending a Catholic school:

> Although Catholic dogma and Catholic hierarchy informed this regime of power, authority, and control, I saw no significant difference between these practices and those of other Christian power structures that also enforced binaries of good/bad, self/other, male/female, gay/straight, and Christian/heathen, while giving so-called religious leaders a cover for immorality and bigotry. Very early on, I was a humanist and a feminist without necessarily having the language to break it down that way. Being humanist and feminist demands questioning received dogmas and slaying

sacred cows whose very existence depends on your erasure. To subscribe to a human-centered notion of morality, ethics, and justice as a Black woman is an outlier position that carries social, political, and professional risks.[5]

What should be acknowledged, what this book calls attention to, is the unlikely resident—Black humanism—in the house of meaning-making. This is simply to say, again, that there is an impressive number of Black Americans who claim no particular (theistic) religious orientation—but (and here's the kicker) they aren't nihilistic, and they aren't hiding away in dark corners feeding on despair. No—they are making their way through the world with community, with a philosophy of life, and in light of certain ritual practices, all of which shape their existence in relationship to others, and in the world.

PLACING BLACK HUMANISM

When it comes to identifying Black humanism, it has often been done by negation: we know what it isn't. (This, for instance, would be a case in which the Black humanist might highlight their atheism, or their attention to science and critical thought, in which case they might emphasize their freethought or skepticism.) Without doubt, its range of interests and social critiques would mean it isn't synonymous with the humanism coming out of the Enlightenment, in part because it challenges some key Enlightenment assumptions concerning the nature and meaning of the human, the workings of race, and so on. It isn't theistic in orientation, and, although some individuals remain within the community of Black theists, it isn't a dimension of the Black Church tradition. To the contrary, there are signs that Black humanism exists in opposition to the Black Church. Yet there are similarities with Black churches—overlapping concerns, so to speak. For example, despite the rhetoric of some of its more atheistic advocates, Black humanism concerns itself with meaning-making. In noting this, I am not suggesting that it is concerned with transhistorical relationships; rather, this is to say that Black humanism, like various forms of Black theism (e.g., Black churches, Black Islamic orientations, certain modes of Black Buddhism, voodoo, Lucumi) seeks to answer the fundamental questions of human existence, such as, Who are we? What are we? Why are we? When are we? These speak to concerns and probing having to do with the desire to make life meaningful—to make meaning of one's existence.

In addition, although it doesn't associate such questioning with revelation or special knowledge, Black humanism offers ways to ritualize its wrestling with these questions: it develops language and practices that are meant to capture and repeat their significance and the accompanying answers. In this way, Black humanists, like their theistic neighbors, reframe time and space so as to commemorate certain things about human life and to do so in the context of the like-minded, or what we might call "community." Some of this ritualizing involves effort to distinguish themselves from Black theists, as well as from white humanists, for whom the range of motivations and concerns can be different (i.e., for the former what it means to be part of a marginalized and racially defined population, and for the latter what it means to exists within a context of privilege). When done in community, this Black humanist work is also meant to offer a "soft place to land"—a new community, a new way of communicating life aims and concerns free of a god-based language of life. This suggests that Black humanism can constitute an alternate space, a different framing of life that maintains the awe and wonder associated with transhistorical claims found in theism(s), *but* in such a way as to ground them in the materiality of physical life. As Asher_Jak reflects, "When I lost my belief in the supernatural, I gained a deep sense of wonder for the naturalistic world. I stopped being afraid of what could happen and started appreciating what has happened."[6]

These similarities and differences with Black churches and other forms of Black religion raise questions about how one might rightly categorize or label Black humanism. Does all of this make Black humanism a religion? Are Black humanists involved in the religious practice of disbelief?

BLACK HUMANISM AS A RELIGIOUS MOVEMENT

Some time ago—and I continue to believe this naming is legitimate—I argued that humanism in general and Black humanism in particular qualify as a religious orientation or system.[7] As one might imagine, this didn't go over so well in most circles of "nonbelievers" but was viewed as a misnaming, a misunderstanding, or, at worst, a betrayal.

There is a visceral reaction—a reluctance or downright refusal—on the part of many humanists to humanism being called a "religion." This is due to an assumption that religion is reducible to the theistic modes of expression they've rejected. What I suggest here, however, isn't equating humanism with theism. Instead, I'm suggesting that religion is simply a tool, a technology, a device for examining human experience—with the intention of finding some type of meaning that connects the individual to something more than the individual. This understanding of religion doesn't assume a god or gods, and it doesn't require a heavenly gaze; it entails a structure of thought and practice aiming to locate and unpack life-meaning. This definition frees religion from *theo*logy and serves to recognize the various ways in which meaning-making (i.e., the work of religion) is fostered without god(s). As I hope becomes clear over the course of the following pages, Black humanism can be appreciated as a (secular) religious orientation: a way to examine and name human experience so as to discern from it the nature and meaning of (Black) human life. Based on this definition, humanism—even secular humanism—is a religious system in that it is used to explore human experience and foster some sort of meaning for the individual or community doing the looking. When this life-meaning is tied to ethical commitments, one might say, as some following Thomas Paine have said: "To do good is my religion." This is not to say that one *must* understand Black humanism this way—rather, that thinking Black humanism within this broader sense of religion might offer a way to better understand and process some of its functions and community building efforts.

To reiterate an important point, strong negative reactions to this sort of labeling represent a misunderstanding of the nature and meaning of religion. Opponents assume it to be already and always defined by theistic beliefs. This reaction is premised on the assumption that calling Black humanism a religion is to render it indistinguishable from theism. Yet there is a distinction, a significant difference, between theism and religion: the former entails attention to God or gods that conditions the nature and meaning of human existence by tying it to transhistorical claims and often a special knowledge available only to those in line with the wishes and aims of the divine. The Black Church is theistic; the Nation of Islam is theistic; and so are voodoo, Lucumi, and numerous other orientations found within Black communities. Black humanism, however, is not. Religion is simply a tool for exploring experience, a method for making life meaningful—it requires no attention to God or gods. In short: all forms of theism are religion, but not all religion is theistic.

Furthermore, Black humanism modifies and transforms existing ("old") structures. I want to understand it as a relatively new or recent religious movement in several ways. It is a new or recent religious movement in that it (1) seeks to correct and reframe humanism as it emerged during the modern period and does so based on social codes amplified by developments marking modernity; and (2) it highlights the practices and thinking of a typically excluded population. The former places Black humanism on a timeline of development—with "new" entailing both location and intent to carve out a different relationship of Blacks to the social (and natural) world of which they are a part. And it does so by challenging ontological assumptions made regarding people of African descent intellectually reinforced through the anti-Blackness informing much (humanist) thought during the Enlightenment. Black humanism challenges the widespread assumption that people of African descent are less than human, with reduced capacities and limited ability for fruitful sociopolitical interactions; it counters this perspective not through a robust theological anthropology, but through a more secular (e.g., scientific and philosophical) claim to full humanity. In this way, Black humanism works to reconfigure and expand the category of the human and, in so doing, to deny the truth of anti-Black racism's claims to the contrary. Furthermore, it seeks to make visible the thought and cultural practices that distinguish a certain segment of the Black population from communities of theism. Black humanism detangles Black thought and practice from the stranglehold of church-based praxis, and, in the process, it amplifies the cultural forms of Black expression (e.g., folk wisdom, the blues, Harlem Renaissance artistic production, Black realism) that critique—or, at least, challenge—the dominance of theism as the basis for Black self-understanding

WHY THINK ABOUT BLACK HUMANISM AS RELIGION?

To speak about Black humanism as religion and to think about Black humanist communities as religious isn't to degrade Black humanism or its organizations. Instead, it is to acknowledge the depth and range of its impact, its ability to foster life meaning in ways that connect individuals to something greater—in this case, expansive social networks and communities. All of this requires freeing the category of religion from the theistic assumptions that long have held it captive; it entails liberating Black humanism from narrow thinking that limits the ability to appreciate its impact on how we live and what we think about our living. To label it "religion" isn't to trap it in theological quagmire—as if theology is the only way to name the religious, as if philosophy doesn't provide a similarly vital structuring mechanism. It is to recognize (and name) the sense of awe and wonder Black humanism motivates as it pulls people into a deeper sense of themselves—for instance, that which they hold true, the function of connection to those with whom they share this sense of truth(s), and the ethical obligations these truths promote. Although our aims and our thinking on religion aren't identical, I find something of what I mean in the words of writer and activist Candace Gorham, whose appreciation for a grammar of wonder I find compelling, in that it opens space for thinking expansively concerning what Black humanism is. In her book on death, dying, and grief, she writes,

> I have grown to like "nontheist" as a broad-spectrum term that carries less baggage than more commonly used words such as "atheist" or "agnostic." And because discussions about death are often virtually inseparable from discussions about the spiritual, I intentionally wanted to use a term with direct spiritual implications—unlike terms such as "secular" or "freethinker," which more generally speak to social and civic issues.[8]

By "spiritual," Gorham isn't talking about a realm of non-material beings, of transhistorical realities; she is capturing the dimensions of human life that aren't satisfied through the structures of reason. She is referencing a part of us that is more difficult to name. It is this dimension of Black humanism, or what Gorham calls "nontheism," that I want to capture through the language of religion.

The language of atheism doesn't capture these proactive meaning-making tendencies of Black humanism in that it simply highlights what is not embraced. There is more to Black humanism than what Black humanists don't believe or don't do. Again, I use the category of "religion" as a way to highlight and center Black humanism's concern with the fostering of communal frameworks intended to provide a space for meaning-making. The language of religion additionally allows an opportunity to amplify the ritual dimension of Black humanist community—the activities that render time and space special—marking out and celebrating or mourning events. The need for and utility of ritual is recognized, for example, when one is mindful of the presence of Black (atheistic) humanist celebrants or chaplains. For activist and organizer Mandisa Thomas, a humanist celebrant "endorsed by the Humanist Society and the Universal Life Church," gatherings are charged events that have something to do with orchestrating our search for life-meaning and with observing those moments that strike us as profound.[9] As Thomas describes the importance of humanist celebrants: "Humanist celebrants are still a very underserved need in the community of nonreligious people who are leaving their churches and are looking for these services . . . I would say that it was due to my activism that I eventually became a celebrant, and it is just another extension of my work."[10]

DIMENSIONS OF BLACK HUMANISM IN FIVE CHAPTERS

As it stands, this brief presentation of Black humanism might raise more questions than it answers. This is particularly the case in that *real* attention to Black humanism is still fairly young and develops in the shadow of the Black churches most closely associated with the structure of Black communities. Still, in this book, readers will gain a better sense of why it is important to think about Black humanism as a religious movement with deep roots within Black communities.

To accomplish this, the volume is broken down into five chapters. The first chapter explores the principles that animate Black humanism. What I'm calling "principles" are the moral and ethical codes that shape Black humanism and that serve to distinguish it from various theisms at work in Black communities in the United States. Some of these, like a critique of supernatural claims, are explicit in the available literature, while others (e.g., the interconnected nature of all life) require more effort to discern in the cultural production in which Black humanism is often embedded. The second chapter discusses the historical development of Black humanism, moving from the early African presence to the mid-twentieth century. Attention is given to an initial challenge to theism presented through various cultural forms, including songs, folk wisdom, activism, and writings, along with brief consideration of some key figures. The third chapter, which examines Black humanism during the twenty-first century, highlights growth in the number of Black Americans who claim no particular religious affiliation (i.e., Black Nones), which marks a more public self-understanding of Black Americans as nontheists, as non-church-affiliated. The fourth chapter considers the involvement of Black humanism within social justice efforts over the course of several centuries, paying attention to key figures from the mid-twentieth-century civil rights movement and more recent abolitionist efforts such as Black Lives Matter. The final chapter explores various forms Black humanist community has taken and considers why community formation has been important to Black humanists.

In exploring the themes for these chapters, it has been important to me to position readers so they can hear the voices of Black humanists, to hear their stories, by giving as much attention to their actual words as possible. In that way, I serve as a narrator weaving together academic work on Black humanism with the lived experience of Black humanists. To accomplish this, I appeal directly to particular contemporary and historical humanists, and I quote them so that their voices are heard, turning to popular sources that offer a lived context for the more academic materials used. My aim isn't to hide behind these quotations or avoid presenting my own thinking on the various topics highlighted here; readers will find me in these pages as well, as this story of Black humanism is also my story. But I hope readers will leave this book knowing something about the institutional *and* personal dimensions of a layered, complex, and vibrant community—a disbelieving community—helping to reshape what it means to be Black and religious in the United States.

Taken as a whole, this book presents the historical development and praxis of an important but often underappreciated form of Black religion that can't be accounted for through Black churches and other theistic movements. Black humanism is its own thing, so to speak—a form of ritualized Black self-expression as old as the US Black community and with a continued relevance as recent at twenty-first-century abolitionist efforts.

THE **BLACK PRACTICE** OF **DISBELIEF**

CHAPTER 1

PRINCIPLES OF BLACK HUMANISM

For those not familiar with the word, a Humanist is basically an atheist who takes strong moral stances on things, or for whom morality is a clear and present factor in the thoughts and actions in their daily lives.

—KEN GRANDERSON

To the extent that Black humanism can be understood as a new religious movement, it can be said to wrestle with the fundamental questions of human existence and, in the process, offer ways to find and act on life-meaning. In this chapter, we'll turn to the principles that animate and define what Black humanists "believe."

While there is variation, I argue that six principles communicate Black humanism's basic beliefs or tenets and shape its values and ethics: (1) suspicion toward and/or rejection of God concepts; (2) human accountability and responsibility for the human condition tied to an obligation to the larger arena of life; (3) belief in the materiality of life, without attention to theological claims of the soul and life outside human history; (4) human community in relationship to the world as the framework for practice; (5) knowledge as strictly a consequence of logic and reason; and (6) perpetual improvement as necessary.

NO GOD(S)

Stepping back from theism's claims to god(s) present and concerned with the well-being of humanity, Black humanism focuses on the human. However, this is not a radical optimism that fails to account for the great harm done through human reason and by means of the human capacity for mischief. Black humanism is well aware of the various ways people of African descent have been misnamed, marginalized, and dehumanized, all justified by an appeal to the assumed superiority of Europeans and their narrative of a grand destiny. It is far too cognizant of this potential for harm to embrace an uncritical praise of humanity of any color; instead, its attention to humanity is meant to suggest concern with the subjectivity and integrity of life over against policies that render particular groups dominant. Furthermore, Black humanism's position regarding notions of divinity and its embrace of humanity is meant to shift attention away from unchallenged justifications for activity and practices—including modes of thinking—tied to structures of capital "T" truth instituted by grand "Others." This is an important move for Black humanists because there are graphic examples of the God concept being used to justify abuse of Black bodies and warping of minds, with Black theists playing along. For example, many Black church theologies raise the question of theodicy: What can be said about God in light of human suffering in the world? Determined to maintain the notion of a just, kind, compassionate, and capable God, these theologies reason that Black suffering must have a purpose. Therefore, in various forms, such theologies promote theories of redemptive suffering—which is to say, out of Black suffering God will bring about a wonderful good because suffering is either justified punishment for wrongdoing, a pedagogical tool to advance Black people through powerful lessons, or a mystery that God will reveal over time.

One can imagine that redemptive suffering arguments made it difficult to strictly identify racial injustice as an evil in the world because God might be using it to punish or to teach. And how could an action on the part of a good God not be good . . . in the long run? Nonetheless, from the blues onward, this sense of divinely sanctioned suffering has raised questions for many concerning the utility of this God idea: Of what value was it if it served merely to sanction their misery? There was another way, some reasoned, to explain the suffering of Black people—that there is no God. There is no substantive evidence, the counterargument goes, to justify theistic claims regarding the divine. What one does see are humans causing misery and pointing their fingers toward the sky or toward the Bible to sanction their aims. The suffering of Black people is tied to greed, white-supremacist aims, and to the preservation of white privilege in its various forms, and, because they are human in origin, these sources of misery can be critiqued and dismantled. Such a position freed Blacks from confinement to unchallenged theological claims concerning the structure of the universe and enhanced their sense of themselves as subjects, rather than objects, of history. Finally, there is the belief that humans aren't created by some divine force as narrated in the Hebrew Bible and advanced by the Christian Testament, the Quran, and other theistic texts. Humans are the result of an evolutionary process, and the earth is explained scientifically through the big bang, not through the magic of cosmic forces.

HUMAN ACCOUNTABILITY AND RESPONSIBILITY

Humans construct the circumstances they encounter and author justifications for that behavior. In other words, they are accountable and responsible for the human condition. But human wants can't be the litmus test that determines all; human need is to be placed in relationship with the needs of the larger ecosystem of which humans are only a part. As a consequence, a sense of ecological responsibility prevents a "human as the measure of all things" posture toward the world, or an assumption that all exists for the benefit of humanity. There is no doubt that humans have done great harm, but instead of attempting to tie this to some sort of large-scale, cosmic drama, it is linked exclusively to human wants and desires. The improvement of the quality of life for all requires human action, human work alone. Yet it is important to recognize that human effort doesn't guarantee outcomes, and this is a significant difference between the religious ethics of theists and that of Black nontheists. The former tends to assume that their efforts combined with cosmic assistance will bring about the desired results. How could it be otherwise when the most powerful force(s) in the universe are committed to the well-being of the faithful? When there is a delay, or when circumstances seem to intensify in their negative outcomes, theological sleight of hand allows for a continued optimism regarding the future.

This particular Black humanist principle rests on an assumption that human engagement comes with a strong possibility of failure. This realization doesn't cause apathy; rather, it prompts a different orientation—one that assumes nothing. Some read this as a type of nihilism, but those who hold to it do not. To the contrary, for them, it isn't a surrender to circumstances; it urges effort not because it is guaranteed to have an effect but because human action is our last and best option—in other words, it is all humans can offer, the only thing on which humans can count. If there is something one might call a victory, or that might constitute progress, it is found in the very act of rebellion against injustice. Nothing about this stance entails an assumption that struggle doesn't matter. Human achievement is matched by human failure, human potential matched by human disappointment. This recognition isn't assumed a tragedy. To a certain extent, it is simply understood as part of the meaning of human life. Instead of nihilism, one might call it a type of godless realism—a sense that history tells us something about the nature and meaning of human engagement with each other and the world. This is a fundamental commitment to the world, and the human's place in it. Patterns of conduct written across the years mean something, and they point only to our presence, not to a mystical presence unaccounted for through reason and inquiry.

HISTORY AND EMBODIMENT

For the Black humanist, there is the materiality of life without attention to theological claims regarding existence of the soul and life outside the framework of human history. Black theists argue for something beyond the physical—a world of spiritual beings impinging on human life. For many, this is tied to a theological argument for the human being as more than its physical form in that the body is simply the housing for a spiritual substance that connects humans to the spirit world; it is the soul that must be recognized and nurtured through proper thinking and doing. Black Christians, even the most progressive who see only figurative or symbolic value in biblical teachings, have been known to position themselves among those who believe the physical a poor reflection of more important metaphysical considerations. Sunni Islam notes a reality beyond it, and members of the Nation of Islam give name to a special knowledge and to transhistorical realities. Practitioners of voodoo and Lucumi, in addition, recognize cosmic forces—some personified—that inform and influence human life.

For Black humanists, however, there is nothing after physical death. At best, we remain "alive" only in the memories of those whose lives we touched during our living. Instead of seeing the body as a mere casing for and a hindrance to the soul, the Black humanist understands embodiment as central to it. This isn't to say that the body lacks an animated quality, that there isn't a mind and patterns of unseen events, chemical reactions, and the like that make the body alive. But none of these inner workings (many of them not fully understood) point to a cosmic force or creator. Instead, for the Black humanist, the mysteries of the human body and human life are worked out through science and reason. Neither "sacred" texts like the Bible or the Quran, nor stories of origins such as those associated with the *Odus* of Ifa appeal to the Black humanist as theological truth—they are considered humanly contrived stories that misname sources. For the Black humanist, stories are important cultural considerations that tell us something about ourselves—our fears, aims, goals, sources of meaning, and more—but the framework for embodied human meaning-making is shaped in and by human history.

This turn to materiality, to the significance of embodiment, doesn't wipe out the possibility of wonder and awe, a particular type of reverence, for the Black humanist. Instead of this wonder or reverence being directed at gods and other spiritual forces, it is tied to the mysteries of the world—the beautiful and tremendous power of the physical universe, which serves as a reminder that humans are a small part of something big and powerful.

COMMUNITY AND WORLD

Black humanists gain perspective and a sense of place through participation in community. There is nothing divine about this engagement, although some might call it "sacred" to the extent that it pulls individuals beyond themselves, forcing recognition of something larger, grander, and with greater capacity then any one person can muster. There is a type of sacredness to this realization, but it is a secular sacredness to the extent that it doesn't entail a statement concerning spiritual forces (e.g., gods, angels, demons), and it doesn't require transhistorical considerations. However, for many Black humanists there is a sense of their ancestors as vital, as a collective forged over the course of centuries. Ancestors are remembered, and they serve as a source of connection to a robust past, a marker of obligation in the present, and so their descendants seek to live in a way that recognizes the sacrifices made by those who came before. A sense of identity, of personhood, of social place, is tied to one's ancestors. In this way, community, inclusive of the deceased, becomes a context for meaning-making, where a sense of self is forged and constituted. Hence, a common question asked within Black gatherings when encountering someone for the first time: Who are your people?

The world is the overarching space within and upon which life takes place for Black humanists. This fosters a concern for environmental renewal and ecological accountability. There is also need to recognize the degree to which Black life has been victimized by white supremacy and used to foster ecological devastation. The relationship is a complicated one, in that slavery entailed a particular connection to the land devoid of subjectivity and self-determination, and freedom didn't necessarily change this connection in significant ways. In short, Black Americans are both victims and victimizers. As Alice

Walker makes clear, in *Living by the Word* as well as other texts, a humanist sensibility needs to include recognition of connectedness to the earth. We are part of the environment, not a distinct reality over against the world.

Furthermore, the Black humanist understanding of the world is scientific in terms of its materiality, and cultural in terms of its sociality. However, a distinction is possible. While earth involves focused attention on the physical environment, the world is more expansive and includes the sociocultural, political, and economic frameworks imposed on the earth. As these are overlapping realities, often the terms are used interchangeably. We are entangled with the materiality of the earth/world—a part of it, dependent on it, and obligated to it. At its best, this sensibility is consistent with the thinking of figures like Walker, in aiming to minimize our negative impact on the world, in recognizing that the web of oppression includes environmental destruction because the same impulse of greed and disregard that sanctioned racial violence gives sanction to ecological harm. And, so, while many Black humanists understand care for the earth and the transformation of the social world as a fundamental dimension of their principles and ethical obligation, they are suspicious to the extent that such work on the part of many does not include an equal commitment to marginalized humans—attention to the treatment of sea life and pets, but disregard for the demise of Black and Brown children.

WHAT WE CAN KNOW

There is no source of special knowledge, no mystical arrangements that produce spiritual gnosis. Instead, there is information that comes from experience lodged in the teachings and wisdom of the ancestors. From folk wisdom during the period of slavery to the more recent writings of figures like Audre Lorde, James Baldwin, Richard Wright, and Toni Morrison, cultural expression has served as an important source of knowledge, helping Black humanists negotiate a tricky social world. The sociocultural lessons they provide can help the careful person negotiate the sociopolitical and economic landscape and, in this way, generate life-meaning. In addition to these sources, science plays a role in shaping what can be known. For Black humanists, this is not without its worries, since science exists within the context of cultural worlds marked and shaped by social norms—in other words, scientific investigation has not been free from racial disregard and bias. Think, for example, of the nineteenth-century pseudosciences that were meant to prove the inferiority of Black people: measuring head size and body symmetry blurred the boundary between subjective preference and scientific evidence and allowed for the ranking of beings, putting Europeans at the top and people of African descent at the bottom. Such thinking opened Black people to scientifically sanctioned abuse.

Experimentations to advance racial science during and after slavery assumed that Blacks were less than human, animal-like. More recently, think of the racial bias that informs access to medical technology and advanced treatments. Despite its drawbacks, the advantage with science is the ability to critique and challenge assertions because it is this-worldly, whereas spiritual gnosis, because of its assumed transhistorical source, rests safely outside any substantive verification or challenge. This does not mean that the biblical text, for instance, has no meaning for Black humanists. Some do appreciate its aesthetic and its poetic qualities, and some might even make use of biblical materials in crafting their sense of the world and their place in it. However, this doesn't constitute an embrace of the Bible's theological claims—rather, an appreciation of its style of presentation.

PERPETUAL IMPROVEMENT

Black humanism is porous, which is another way of saying it is open to influence and alteration. In this openness is found one of its strengths. Black humanists believe that their humanism must shift and change over time in relationship to a growing sense of what it means to be Black and a humanist in a country showing ever more intense forms of disregard.

Black humanism isn't a tradition, if what is meant by "tradition" is a static mode of thought and practice based on signs and symbols, structures of meaning and exchange, that are fixed and self-revelatory. Critique within that sort of tradition is met typically with resistance built into the system's self-understanding as premised on unchanging *Truth* given in relationship to the workings of a "Grand Other." For Black humanism, there is a sense of evolution—a shift and change over time connected to the fluid nature of need and a growing sense of one's relationship to self and others. While not always achieving it, Black humanism is committed to self-awareness. Tied to this is a sense that one's humanity isn't fixed but rather entails organic and reactive connections. To remain stationary is a failure to maximize human potential. Whereas many Black Christians might think in terms of perfection, or the perfectibility of humanity through divine interaction (which in some ways is the point of acting out one's faith), Black humanism resists such claims, recognizing instead that perfection isn't the goal. Black humanism instead aims for improvement: the presence of possibility by means of which there is a continued striving toward better relationships, improved life conditions, and a healthy earth. Black humanism seeks "more"—an enhancement of humanity's best abilities, all the while recognizing that humans will fall sort of their desires. This perspective is tied to an appreciation for uncertainty.

Unlike many Black theists, Black humanists are not troubled by the vulnerability that uncertainty entails. How could theists who count on suprahuman assistance be consistently at ease with instability? Such comfort might fly in the face of a reliance on powers not subject to human shortcomings. For Black humanists, reliance on human ingenuity and capacity can't wipe out uncertainty; instead, uncertainty is recognized as a moral value and an ethical reality, a basis from which one works, that motivates action and enlivens a sense of possibility. Human frailty isn't a metaphysical concern addressed by transcendent means; it is simply a fact, one that is addressed through a perpetual effort to be better, to do better, to improve while acknowledging that these efforts will fall short in significant ways.

As many Black humanists have acknowledged and advanced as part of the larger agenda, this attention to evolution—sensitivity to circumstances and an effort to rethink the workings of humanism so as to meet changing needs—requires attention to a variety of issues often underappreciated within Black communities, like mental health. In general, mental health education and practice has been a challenge within these communities. But a principle of productive change requires attention to what might hamper an individual's ability to adapt and progress.

▲ ▲ ▲ ▲ ▲ ▲ ▲ ▲ ▲ ▲ ▲

CHAPTER 2

A BRIEF (RELIGIOUS) HISTORY OF BLACK HUMANISM

And godless though I am, the fact of being human, the fact of possessing the gift of study, and thus being remarkable among all the matter floating through the cosmos, still awes me.

—TA-NEHISI COATES

Black humanism in the United States is as old as the Black population itself. Although denied access to reading and writing, enslaved Africans forged forms of cultural production that spoke with as much power as a written text. Elements of what we would come to call "Black humanism" in these early forms of cultural expression grew in detail and complexity as Black Americans pushed for freedom. As discussed in the previous chapter, what it involves held significance for many and would guide their lives before they claimed the label, if they ever did. The way Black humanists named themselves at any given time (freethinkers, skeptics, humanists, atheists, agnostics) would expand, depending on what particular aspect of their humanistic identity they meant to highlight. Mindful of this, Ken Granderson's twenty-first-century claim reflects this situation, which dates back centuries: "It is safe to say that I've been a Humanist my entire life—long before I ever learned the word."[1]

Black humanism within its various incarnations gained institutional form during the early twentieth century as Black Americans participated in rethinking the political and economic life of the United States, post-reconstruction. For instance, organized systems of thought and practice such as Unitarianism and, later, Unitarian Universalism and communism provided home or grounding for some Black humanists. All of this, over time, would attest to a growing and vibrant nontheistic approach to self-understanding and meaning-making forged during the period of slavery and extending into the twentieth century, solidified by the development of communal forms of engagement.

EARLY CULTURAL PRODUCTION

Signs of a disposition and mode of thought that reflects what we have come to call "Black humanism" can be seen in early critiques of Christian assumptions and sensibilities. Think, for instance, of the blues. Rather than beginning with "race records" and artists of the early twentieth century, think a longer history, for, as many scholars have argued, we can't accurately date the emergence of the form. During the period of slavery, one gathers a sense that for some blues musicians theological claims grounded in the idea of a God at work in the world ring hollow. Instead of operating in accordance with faith, these blues tunes made assertions about life in light of existential circumstances and the response of Black bodies to those circumstances. They made light of claims concerning a benevolent God, they challenged the moral and ethical codes of Christian community members, and they advanced a sense of life grounded in materiality. What churches frowned upon the blues embraced. Sex, dancing, the erotic possibilities of illicit joy—all were met with graphic depiction and celebration. Years later, Muddy Waters would capture some of this counter-Christian irreverence when tying his sexual prowess to possession of items associated with hoodoo. In the song "Hoochie Coochie Man," he claims that these things (e.g., Johnny Conquer root and a black cat bone) give him a power hard to resist.

The blues speak not only against what was often witnessed in a Black Christian context, but also against whites who held Africans in slavery while declaring themselves God-fearing Christians. As the contradiction between their historical practices and their claims to a transhistorical grace was too rich to ignore, many enslaved and free Africans critiqued and denounced the religion of hypocritical whites and uncritical Blacks who mimicked the beliefs of their oppressors. The blues offered an alternative arrangement of life, embraced and chronicled well beyond the Emancipation Proclamation. Ralph Ellison hints at this idea when reflecting on LeRoi Jones's (Amiri Baraka) book *Blues People*:

> There are levels of time and function involved here, and the blues which might be used in one place as entertainment (as gospel music is now being used in night clubs and on theatre stages) might be put to a ritual use in another. Bessie Smith might have been a "blues queen" to the society at large, but within the tighter Negro community where the blues were part of a total way of life, and a major expression of an attitude toward life, she was a priestess, a celebrant who affirmed the values of the group and man's ability to deal with chaos.[2]

Beyond the music, folktales and folk wisdom advanced a human-based and historically situated sense of life that avoided the metaphysical claims of theists.[3] Within these tales and wisdom narratives, Black Americans spoke against an unjust system, arguing for a sense of life that avoids efforts to find answers to existential concerns through a turn to the "great beyond." Instead, life was interpreted and advanced along the horizontal plain of ordinary encounters and possibilities grounded in what the senses could decipher and advance. These stories—often told using various animals, like Brer Rabbit—signified what it wasn't always safe to say directly. Moreover, they provided an earthy logic that allowed enslaved and free Africans to exercise creativity and work around restrictions through ingenuity and human creativity rather than reliance on cosmic aid that would never come. These stories told of bodies occupying time and space, moving through the world, and they privileged the pain and pleasures associated with those bodies.

One thing that stands out with these folktales, and that I want to highlight here, is laughter—a twisting of circumstances that draws out and tames terror and trauma. Laughter allows for a portion of the community's humanity, worth, and well-being to take center stage by denying the "serious" nature of claims to the contrary. The harshness of life—symbolized in many of these stories as the briar patch—is reenvisioned as a place of possibility. Viewed this way, the laughter often induced through these tales lies outside the bounds of polite society, which makes it consistent with the demand for life-meaning by a despised population. Much, but certainly not all, of Black theism trades on somber affective responses to circumstances, with joy that is measured and always vulnerable to sadness due to the state of the human soul. But with these tales, laughter speaks a different positioning. I turn again to Ellison, whose perspective on comedy—and one can consider these tales a form of early Black comedic presentation—is akin to what I am claiming about the function of laughter. "For by allowing us to laugh at that which is normally unlaughable," he writes, "comedy provides an otherwise unavailable clarification of vision that calms the clammy trembling which ensues whenever we pierce the veil of conventions that guard us from the basic absurdity of the human condition."[4] What it meant to be human was framed in terms of all the mind could dream up, and all the body could secure.

ADVOCATES

Again, while Black Americans didn't necessarily label their philosophy of life "humanism"—instead often using the label of "freethinker," in line with white luminaries and advocates for social transformation such as Robert Ingersoll (1833–1899)—they presented their vantage point by negation. They weren't Christians, and they didn't belong to a church. This position was recognized and lamented by early Black church leaders, like Alexander Payne (b. 1811), who viewed this rejection of God as a sign that slavery and the larger political system served only to damage spiritual well-being. Yet, for those rejecting the church, this nontheistic position spoke to the humanity of enslaved and free Africans by denying the dehumanizing intent of racialized theism. To speak their worth, they were willing to deny the existence of cosmic forces. Historian of Black freethought Christopher Cameron provides various examples, none more impressive than an attorney known as "Mr. Carr" who announced during a 1903 speech at the Manhattan Liberal Club that "the colored race is beginning to feel that not only are all legal enactments and constitutions a farce and delusion, but that Christian civilization is a farce and a snare."[5]

As reflected in the words of Mr. Carr, most nontheistic thinking was found with individuals lacking significant organizational infrastructure until the early twentieth century. There are various reasons for this, including a general limitation on humanist organizing in the United States, as well as racism within white humanist circles. In addition, open disbelief could result in isolation and stigma because of the strength of Black Christian churches. To be Black in the United States already involved a series of challenges: Would Black Americans want to increase their marginalization based on adherence to a stigmatized religious position? While this was an important consideration, one that would continue to have bearing on the visibility of Black humanism, mass movements such as the Communist Party offered a platform and community from which to express anti-theism and more humanistic sensibilities. Consistent with communist assumptions that theism in general and Christianity in particular did little to alleviate the suffering of the marginalized, Black communists rejected the church and sought to advance socio-political and economic interests of Black Americans through organizing and activism. No spiritual renewal, no calls for austere living to secure heaven, just effort to secure socio-economic and political advantage in the here and now! A significant figure within the Black community of socialists and communists was Hubert Harrison (1883–1927), an agnostic who saw the Socialist Party as offering something of value to those who, for too long, were abused and misled by the Christian church. His perspective on this situation is biting:

> It should seem that Negroes, of all Americans, would be found in the Freethought fold since they have suffered more than any other class of Americans from the dubious blessings of Christianity. It has been well said that the two great instruments for the propagation of race prejudice in America are the Associated Press and the Christian Church. This is quite true.[6]

On the theism side, a handful of ministers—for instance, Reverdy C. Ransom (1861–1959) of the African Methodist Episcopal Church—embraced democratic socialism as more in line with the teachings of Jesus Christ. Black socialists and communists who denied the church called for a radical change that gave the means of production, and the benefits of that production, to the workers. One gets a sense of this in a poem by Walter Everette Hawkins (b. 1883), published in the *Messenger*—one of the significant outlets for Black free-thought meant to challenge "traditional religious ideas" while working to advance "'scientific radicalism' among blacks."[7] Hawkins writes,

> *There is too much talk of heaven,*
> *Too much talk of golden streets,*
> *When one can't be sympathetic,*
> *When a needy neighbor meets;*
> *Too much talk about riches*
> *You expect to get "up there,"*
> *When one will not do his duty*
> *As a decent Christian here.*[8]

This turn to a godless system privileging human experience and need was short-lived, as Black Americans realized that attention to the class system didn't mean significant and transformative attention to issues of racial injustice. Racism remained a limited and marginal consideration for most White communists, who argued that addressing class would allow all other needs to fall into place. Nevertheless, what one sees with Black communists is organized and vocal rejection of theism without apology. Earlier signs of humanistic sensibilities were expressed outside any framework of a counter-organization. Cultural creativity and expression is fundamentally groundless; it requires no communal infrastructure other than folks willing to hear a song, or repeat a story. Thus, music and folktales spread an anti-theist message with something like a "do your thing" attitude, while Black communists pushed to forge a network of the like-minded operating in the public arena to advance a shared, written agenda.

HARLEM RENAISSANCE AND BEYOND

Much Black American literature up until the Harlem Renaissance sought to present Black life in a way that pointed out the damage done by racial discrimination and advanced a story of Black Americans as deserving full inclusion in the life of the country, as defined by white norms of sociality. To accomplish this, early Black narratives resisted a full depiction of Black life. Instead, they sought to project only the best—meaning those that could be read in line with white social sensibilities. These narratives argued that departures from these standards were due to discrimination prohibiting the development of the best capacities of Black Americans. This approach to personhood changed with the Harlem Renaissance, an artistic movement spreading from Harlem, on New York City's Manhattan Island, through areas such as Washington, DC, from the late 1910s to, roughly, the end of the 1930s.

For Harlem Renaissance artists, both visual and literary, advocacy for Black humanity involved pushing against the politics of respectability. Anything short of a full and vibrant presentation of Black life in all its complexities, joys, and sorrows was to limit Black Americans to a white idea of Blackness and render them one-dimensional for the comfort of a white audience. This move toward complexity also involved recognition that not all Black life is associated with the moral and ethical sensibilities of Black churches; in fact, much of this literature is critical of the Black Church, exposing its inconsistencies, such as preaching a moral code that isn't upheld by church members or leaders. In these stories, ministers aren't the heroes but are flawed individuals weighed down by trauma and adherence to the very worst principles of the social world.

Novelist and essayist Zora Neale Hurston's depictions of relationships and communities demonstrate the pitfalls and promise of collectivities and mark out violent race, gender, and class-based encounters. What readers get with Hurston (1891–1960) is recognition of the cultural world(s) of Black theism(s) without the assumption that one must embrace it; vocabulary and grammar, signs and symbols, can be engaged without requiring conversion. Reflecting the same thinking, James Weldon Johnson (1871–1938) could note his conversion to disbelief and still write in *God's Trombones* (1927) a moving ode to the Black sermonic style and imagery. Hurston and

Johnson serve as two examples of how the Harlem Renaissance often disentangled language from practice and, in this way, tamed the claims of theism, while using its grammar of wonder. In their work, language is simply a system of cultural signifiers that can be put to secular use to describe not spiritual commitment but imagination along the horizontal frame of life. Hurston could present, with energy and respect, forms of theism practiced by Black Americans in the Deep South without claiming personally a sense of their spiritual authority and power. She understood why some claim belief in god(s), but such a claim doesn't seem of personal importance to her—although, at times, she participated in theistic activities as an anthropologist attempting to understand the dynamics of Black life. On a personal level, there's reason to believe that Hurston was content to use the resources available to her, those that had a certain materiality. "So," she writes, "I do not pray. I accept the means at my disposal for working out my destiny . . . Prayer is for those who need it. Prayer seems to me a cry of weakness, and an attempt to avoid, by trickery, the rules of the game as laid down. I do not choose to admit weakness. I accept the challenge of responsibility."[9]

This artistic depiction of life that didn't assume the centrality of theism but, rather, explored human existence from the vantage point of human history and experience, is not limited to literature. The visual and performative arts also expressed Black life through a focused presentation on embodied, mundane encounters that frame and highlight human meaning as earthy. For example, "The Banjo Lesson" by Henry Tanner (1859–1937) presents the values of human existence, the nature of relationship, not in terms of verticality—that is, interaction between the divine and humanity—but through intimate encounter and human cooperation, as an elder teaches a young child how to make music.

Much of what I've presented to this point involves humanist-leaning sensibilities, but a forceful shift toward an explicit humanism takes place post-Renaissance, during what might be called "the period of Black realism." When thinking of this period, one should keep in mind the work of literary figures such as Nella Larsen (1891–1965), Richard Wright (1908–1960), and James Baldwin (1924–1987). Some have argued that cultural production during this period maintained a connection to Black Christianity, if for no other reason than these figures continued to speak about it, reflect on it, struggle with it, rendering critique simply as a way of stating Black Christianity's value and importance by negation. However, I think this is a weak argument, one that doesn't take seriously the ability to think the world outside the spiritualization of language and intent. It is to assume there is no "outside," no space beyond the influence and reach of Black Christianity. Critique by Black realism can be—and should be—understood as a negation and a movement toward the formation of life opportunity and identity free of theistic assumption.

Larsen, Wright, and Baldwin, among others, announce a new sense of self in relationship to the world; they hold humans accountable and responsible for their circumstances and for improving their life condition.

These authors expose theistic commitment and performance for the damage it does to the integrity of Black personhood. They highlight the manner in which adherence to church values, for example, comes at the expense of human health and well-being as suffering gets cast as the marker of human advancement and divine engagement. Church devotion destroys productive human relationships, as Larsen's novel *Quicksand* (1928) makes explicit. Helga Crane, the main character, moves from social disregard on the part of whites, and some Blacks, to an embrace of Black theism in the form of a country preacher and his church, only to encounter a death-dealing arrangement in which her value is reduced to the children her body produces. Prayer and service to the church do nothing but enhance her misery, and she eventually realizes why: God, and, therefore, God's assistance, are an illusion. Crane is left to her own devices, responsible for her own well-being, and accountable for her own happiness. As she is contemplating her condition—namely, a church community that hates her, a husband who only values her reproductive capacity, and children that consume her strength, "within her emaciated body raged disillusion. Chaotic turmoil. With the obscuring curtain of religion rent, she was able to look about her and see with shocked eyes this thing that she had done to herself. She couldn't, she thought ironically, even blame God for it, now that she knew that He didn't exist."[10] While not named as such explicitly, there is to be found in her resolve elements of the humanist principles presented in the first chapter of this book.

In his nonfiction, including his memoirs *Black Boy* (1945) and *American Hunger* (1977), Richard Wright calls for humanism as a way to advance beyond the stagnation of human opportunity and creativity represented by racism and reenforced through the antihuman theologizing of theism—that is, Black churches. Better known than his nonfiction are works of fiction like *Native Son* (1940) and *The Man Who Lived Underground* (1941/42). Wright pushes against a theistically arranged set of values that urge obedience over critical thinking, and that diminish self-worth for the sake of heaven. Wright calls for engagement with the material conditions of life—a rebellion against injustice that recognizes human accountability for the condition of the world, while noting that struggle against injustice may not be enough to end it. This stance is present in autobiographical form in *Black Boy*, where he reflects on his grandmother's church:

Many of the religious symbols appealed to my sensibilities and I responded to the dramatic vision of life held by the church, feeling that to live day by day with death as one's sole thought was to be so compassionately sensitive toward all life as to view all men as slowly dying, and the trembling sense of fate that welled up, sweet and melancholy, from the hymns blended with the sense of fate that I had already caught from life. But full emotional and intellectual belief never came. Perhaps if I had caught my first sense of life from the church I would have been moved to complete acceptance, but the hymns and sermons of God came into my heart only long after my personality had been shaped and formed by unchartered conditions of life. I felt that I had in me a sense of living as deep as that which the church was trying to give me, and in the end, I remained basically unaffected.[11]

Rather than theistic optimism, Wright exposes hypocrisy. The church says things will change because God says so. Wright, in response, mocks such misguided thinking and calls for defiance as its own reward. While Black Christians speak of the great "by and by"—with death overcome through spiritual obedience—Wright asserts that there is nothing after death, and a painful death often comes despite our best efforts to pursue transformative values. Unlike his Christian counterparts, for Wright the world is without reason; it shows no concern for humans, and it doesn't respond to their questions, wants, and needs. As he recounts in *Black Boy*, Wright tried, at the request of his grandmother, to embrace the Christian faith, and, had he encountered theistic religion before the world, he would have been able to believe. But the harshness of the world, the conditions of Black life, made it impossible to embrace the unfounded claims and violent demands of Christian practice.

James Baldwin, on the other hand, grew up in the Pentecostal Church. As he recounts in *Go Tell It on the Mountain* (1953), he pursued ministry as a way to shift the power dynamics in his home, which was run by an overbearing father. Moreover, because in Harlem everyone had to belong to something or someone, for him it might as well be the church.[12] However, that theistic community offered limited comfort and, with respect to his sexual urges, only fostered trauma; his sense of himself and his relationship to the larger world were warped by the puritanical demands of a religious community that failed to meet its own expectations. Baldwin eventually left the church, and, although he maintained some of the wonder he gained first in relationship to the theologizing of the church, his aims and orientation became more secular, more humanistic. One gets a sense of this in *The Fire Next Time* (1963) as he reflects on a visit with the Honorable Elijah Muhammad of the Nation of Islam.[13] Baldwin worried that he might be asked about his own faith commitment; he didn't want to have to tell the leader of the Nation of Islam that he wasn't part of the church any longer, but that writing—one might say human creativity—was his religion.

It had replaced the church and all the church entailed. This dissatisfaction with the church, with all its shortcomings and harmful ways, was present even before he claimed writing. In his words:

> And the blood of the Lamb had not cleansed me in any way whatever. I was just as black as I had been the day that I was born. Therefore, when I faced a congregation, it began to take all the strength I had not to stammer, not to curse, not to tell them to throw away their Bibles and get off their knees and go home and organize, for example, a rent strike.[14]

This type of turn from Christianity in particular and theism in general is also a component of the Black Arts Movement, with figures like LeRoi Jones (Amiri Baraka, 1934–2014) who raised questions concerning the existence of God. The Black Church and other forms of Black theism offered nothing that they found compelling, that explained or challenged the suffering that marked Black life in the United States. Drawing on the energy and aesthetics of Black Power, these artists in literature, visual expression, and performance explored the dynamics of life in terms of its materiality in the here and now. They gave no credence to prospects of another world, or spiritual renewal. They were content to limit themselves to an expression of the joys and pains of life as

Blacks encounter it. In other words, these artists didn't look beyond this world for motivation or guidance; they pored through the stuff of the world—the dance, the singing, the clothing, the jokes, the foods, the warmth of community—for the values that should rightly guide them and other Black people. For these advocates of Black life's complexity and richness over against the toxic qualities of white supremacy, a humanity-inclined approach to life afforded mental freedom and creativity, if nothing more.

NAMING BLACK HUMANISM

Figures like Richard Wright wrote about the value of humanism, but it was a minister in the Unitarian Universalist Association (UUA), Dr. William R. Jones (1933–2012), who offered what was arguably the first systematic presentation of Black humanism. Teaching at Yale Divinity School, Jones produced a series of articles followed by the groundbreaking text *Is God a White Racist? A Preamble to Black Theology* (1973). The sharpest elements of his critique were aimed at his academic colleagues who were committed to the Black Church and working to rethink church theology in light of Black Power and the civil rights struggle. For these radical Black Christians, the idea was to read the Christian story as a narrative of justice for the marginalized led by God in human flesh—the Black Messiah and revolutionary Jesus Christ. Although this thinking disrupted the assumptions of white privilege and white supremacy as grounding for Christian thought and practice, for Jones it did little to wrestle with some of the urgent and underlying issues crushing the joy out of Black existence. For example, the theological claim of a God who sides with the (Black) oppressed fails to adequately address the issue of theodicy discussed in chapter 1. As a reminder, theodicy presents a central question: What can be said about God in light of human suffering? According to Jones, the historical evidence to which these Christian theologians pointed could just as easily indicate that God dislikes Black people and seeks their eradication. Can't ongoing anti-Black racism and all forms of racial disregard outlined in the history of the United States point to this dislike just as easily as it can be shifted to justify claims of divine favor? Hence, the evidence provided by these Black Christian theologians can support a range of arguments, not all of which cohere with claims of a loving, kind, and just deity. Furthermore, Jones argues that a careful read of Black Christian thought suggests the presence of human "functional ultimacy," which is to say that Blacks play a decisive role in their development, and that this role actually supersedes any consideration for divine beings. Jones ultimately advocates for Black humanism as a more productive and historically sound philosophy of life for Black Americans—in fact, he calls it a religion, but one that doesn't seek to wipe out the Black Church but, rather, serves the needs of those for whom Black churches don't promote a workable liberation strategy. He writes:

> Once the black humanist acknowledges his debt to the black church, honors its past labors in the cause of black freedom, but respectfully declines to further its theistic claims, he must address the charge that his position is alien to the black religious perspective. Behind the charge that black humanism is alien to black religion lies an insidious equation that must be exposed for critical examination: the equation of black religion and black theism.[15]

As one might imagine, there was significant resistance to Jones's argument within Black American circles. Whether or not they were inside a theist community, many believed that his assertion that Blacks might be involved with a demonic deity concerned with their demise flew in the face of centuries of assumptions that God favored them and was working to secure their well-being. The discomfort this produced was more than they could bear. For some, Black humanism, as Jones defined it, placed him outside the Black community because critics assumed, again, that to be Black was to be theistic in orientation, if not Christian in practice. Many argued in not-so-subtle terms that it linked Jones with the Enlightenment project and not with the theological orientation of Black Americans for whom the divine is real, regardless of whether they make any real effort to come to know this transhistorical presence. For Jones, though, Black humanism isn't a simple and uncritical embrace of Enlightenment humanism; it is intimately linked to the history of Black American ideas and is easily located within the blues, folktales, and folk wisdom.

Although there are various perspectives on this, beyond Jones, one could argue that an explicit recognition of Black humanism within Black American arts and letters can be found in Alice Walker's acceptance of the American Humanist Association's Humanist of the Year award. Because the association is clear about its values, highlighting its nonsupernatural orientation and its commitment to human accountability and responsibility, her acceptance of the award suggests that Walker's philosophy of life aligns with that of the organization, perhaps with an even more profound recognition of the human's relationship to the larger web of life. In the essay "The Only Reason You Want to Go to Heaven Is That You Have Been Driven Out of Your Mind" (1997), Walker extends a sense of nontheism that embraces relationships that are horizontal and dependent on the materiality of life; here she explores her religious upbringing and her transition away from a church-based orientation toward nature. As Walker writes: "All people deserve to worship a God who also worships them. A God that made them, and likes them. That is why Nature, Mother earth, is such a good choice."[16]

The push against theism by the likes of Larsen, Baldwin, Wright, and Walker is given a twenty-first-century infusion of urgency in light of the anti-Black racism that claimed Black lives on camera without consequence. It is this state-sanctioned Black death, and the need to explain it to his son, that motivated Ta-Nehisi Coates's *Between the World and Me* (2015). The book's title draws a phrase from Richard Wright, but the reference isn't an empty nod in Wright's direction without claiming an orientation similar to his. The book also contains something of Baldwin's sense of the orienting and meaning-making possibility found in producing the written word. Regarding this, Coates writes: "I have my work. I no longer feel it necessary to hang my head at parties and tell people that I am 'trying to be a writer.' And godless though I am, the fact of being human, the fact of possessing the gift of study, and thus being remarkable among all the matter floating through the cosmos, still awes me."[17] There is a sense of wonder, of (human) potential, that frames his practice of life without reliance on hope for cosmic transcendence. In this way, for Coates, like Baldwin and Wright, writing is a ritual practice that ties him to others and allows him a glimpse into possibilities for living in a tragic world. The racist murder of Black people by police officers without repercussions brought into full relief the violence his son might encounter because he is a Black male—a violence Coates couldn't safeguard against. Like humanism-inclined

Black Americans before him, he found no relief in the idea of God, no resolution in the idea of redemptive suffering, and no reason to believe that church-based faith and related action would save the day. Awareness of our circumstances, a lucid engagement with life in relationship to others—perhaps a type of robust love for life in relationship—is the best we can manage. Although this won't be enough to turn the world, it does say something about our humanity, our value, our meaning in relationship to what matters. And this epistemological recentering is worth something.

Whereas various forms of Black theism are troubled by uncertainty and instead develop teleological arrangements that pull history into some grand unity of meaning, Black humanism as expressed by figures such as Walker and Coates involves the use of human ingenuity and a rugged determination to move through a troubled and troubling world without guarantees. Not divine love but human love allows us to keep something of ourselves in the context of a racialized social world that denies so many so much. This sort of earthiness, this comfort with the discomfort of our tragic history, is also played out in the work of artists like Kara Walker, whose drawings and sculptures amplify the manner in which the signs and symbols of enslavement were meant to dehumanize, to reduce Black life to the materiality of white pleasure and prosperity. Many find her images disturbing in part because of their graphic presentation of the erotic as manipulation of

Black bodies. Yet there is something about her thematic structure and the scope of her work that signifies—as did folktales and the blues before her—the logic of dehumanization and white supremacy by recognizing and presenting for examination the workings of the white social world without its narrative of justification. Something about this work speaks a definite Black identity through the persistence of presence despite death-dealing circumstances.

Artistic production that speaks to Black humanist sensibilities isn't limited to the written word or the visual art found in galleries. Filmmakers like Jeremiah Camara, and his documentary *Holy Hierarchy: The Religious Roots of Racism in America* (2019), provide a critique of Black theism and its relationship to and support for injustice. For Camara, this critique is meant to open a new space for discussing the utility of Black humanism as an alternate orientation with a greater capacity to meet the needs of Black Americans. He considers himself, for instance, to be exposing what he calls the lie of Black Christianity and in this way working to break its dominance over Black Americans, freeing them to hold themselves in higher regard by turning away from a system of judgment and punishment expressed through a theological narrative of crucifixion. His film intends to explore and explain a more reason-based approach to Black life. A question underlies this film: Why would anyone embrace theism when it has served to support the dehumanization of Black people? Camara's answer: one shouldn't. In his view, nontheistic patterns of thought and practice, like Black humanism, provide a better approach to life and offer a meaningfulness that doesn't require participation in one's own demise.

As these various artists demonstrate, an undercurrent of nontheism exists within Black American thought and practice, expressed in a variety of ways, but each with the intent of suggesting and celebrating a more earthy and material engagement with life. While not all of them explicitly use the terminology of Black humanism, they all desire and advance an approach to making life meaningful without reliance on cosmic claims and divine figures.

▲ ▲ ▲ ▲ ▲ ▲ ▲ ▲ ▲ ▲

CHAPTER 3

THE EVOLUTION
OF BLACK HUMANISM

In 2008, African Americans were the least likely to be Nones (19.5%), but by 2020 they were more likely to say that they had no religious affiliation than white or Hispanic respondents (34.9%).

—*CHRISTIANITY TODAY*

In polite conversation, often in connection with getting to know someone, it isn't uncommon within Black American communities to hear this question: "What church do you attend?" The assumption is that the answer provides a wealth of information, such as one's roots in the community, one's moral and ethical sensibilities, one's family history. In a general sense, the question is employed as a litmus test of good standing and trustworthiness.

Many celebrate the Black Church as the first organization developed by and for Black people in North America. Hence, its centrality to Black life has been assumed, with involvement (at least membership) required for Blackness—something of a membership card to the Black community. To not participate was to run the risk of social–cultural isolation, expressed in part through questions regarding one's cultural identity. Black theism in the form of the Black Church and the dynamics of Black life were believed to be so entangled that to name one was, in essence, to name the other. As Sikivu Hutchinson notes,

> often in black cultural production, there is the presumption of faith-based, religious or spiritual world views and experiences that preclude more complex portrayals of black life. The straightjacket of faith, spiritualism and religiosity, is particularly problematic when it comes to black women characters who are allowed none of the nuances of belief and individual license afforded "maverick" male characters."[1]

What Hutchinson says is only amplified if one gathers one's sense of the situation from church-centric sources. Here's the catch: most of the sources assume this church-centric posture.

Think in terms of Oprah Winfrey, who argues that one can't be an atheist and experience a sense of wonder or awe, that those feelings are restricted to a certain spiritual awareness. There is in Winfrey's assumption a "soft" form of marginalization that denies what nontheists claim and recasts them in light of what is familiar to her. David Niose gets at the point this way:

> What is most alarming about Oprah's revelation is that she doesn't even realize its invidiousness. Atheists, to her, don't feel that deep, emotional connection to the universe. She has drawn a circle that includes people of all faiths, but excludes atheists, thereby confirming negative attitudes toward nonbelievers.[2]

But the isolation can be more straightforward and more crude. Take, for example, television personality Steve Harvey's warning to women not to date an atheist because, if a man isn't a theist, "you don't know what his 'moral barometer' is." The disregard isn't limited to dating, however, in that for Harvey anyone who doesn't believe in God, "well, then, to me you're an idiot."[3] For Harvey, to be an atheist isn't simply to choose a different path—no, it's to be without proper moral and ethical commitments; it's to be a social problem and a community outsider. Such a person can't be trusted to uphold good standards, and certainly can't be a loving and nurturing partner for someone interested in being moral and ethical.

Another odd component of this connection of the church to Blackness is that it was easily wiped out if one, for example, held membership in a predominantly white denomination.

Those folks faced not only racial challenges within their churches—because race doesn't go away when one enters the sanctuary—but within the larger Black community their authenticity as culturally Black was also brought into question. One either found a home in one of the Black denominations, or one ran the risk of being marginalized within the context of an already marginalized community—with one's claims to life-meaning challenged by issues of authenticity. Is one *really* Black as verified through (Black) Christian community connections? Jamila Bey unpacks the cultural assumption that has kept theism a central marker of Black identity:

> African Americans have allowed the story to be told that we are a God-fearing people. Our culture dictates—mandates, even—that we be spiritual. Accepting that definition of who we are forces us to defend our blackness should we have doubts about spirituality. Accepting that definition means accepting that to be authentically black is to be religious—wrongly—and that to doubt God is a white thing—wrongly. We let others define us, and we dare not buck that expectation.[4]

INSIDE AND OUTSIDE THE BLACK CHURCH

It is difficult to assess numbers regarding those folks who exist outside theism's grasp, and Black churches gave little consideration to this opposition in the past. Instead, Black churches flipped the theological script, arguing that nonbelievers simply were a sign that Christianity had more work to do within Black communities. More evangelizing! More testifying! At other times, little attention was given to nonbelievers because the number of those raising such questions about the church seemed small and manageable. However, the challenge offered by disbelief ramped up in the late twentieth century, when it could no longer be denied.

Despite consternation to the contrary, the Black Church— the numerically most significant form of Black theism—experienced a decline in membership and participation during the post–civil rights years. This is the irony: while not all Black churches participated in civil rights activism, those that did actually helped to put in place life options and opportunities that would reduce the need for the services Black churches traditionally understood themselves to deliver. Black church-sponsored schools (secondary schools and colleges) weren't the only options; leadership opportunities increased beyond those associated with church work; political involvement was now guaranteed, at least in theory; Black-owned businesses and civic organizations gained access to a larger arena of opportunities; and much more. A combination of new forms of involvement in the socioeconomic life of the United States as a result of civil rights legislation meant that the church was no longer the most viable vehicle for mobility and networking. Combined with the church's rather conservative stance on social issues beyond racism, these other, secular mechanisms for success and meaning resulted in a decrease in church participation.

With the civil rights movement came growth in organized effort to extend justice work beyond race (e.g., Black women encountering gender discrimination and class-based discrimination), and this naturally raised questions concerning the moral and ethical sensibilities of Black churches. They'd been involved to some extent in racial justice work, but beyond that there was a tendency to hold up the Bible and denounce other social concerns. This didn't go unnoticed by Black Americans who suffered because of more than race. The centering of Black men wasn't difficult to see from who pastored, who controlled the finances, which issues were preached from the pulpit and fought outside the sanctuary. The church was not proving itself useful beyond a limited range of concerns, and other Black theistic communities weren't doing much better.

Black Americans began to ask themselves an important question: Why remain within an organization that marginalizes my concerns and preaches against my well-being? Even in these churches, the spiritualized and theologized American Dream excluded them. For others, the prosperity gospel that gained great visibility during the late twentieth century also made a graphic and crude association between the gospel and economic gain. For some prosperity gospel preachers, there seemed to be little distinction between, on the one hand, one's bank account and material holdings, and, on the other, one's spiritual riches. These preachers also tended to avoid issues of social justice, instead encouraging religious commitment to fuel material acquisition. While this theological turn was welcomed in certain quarters because it justified economic–social aspirations, for others it pointed out long-standing problems with Christianity. If the church preached a gospel consistent with US empire building, could the church actually save anyone? If not, why be a part of it?

For those raising such questions, theoretical alternatives offered by anticolonial thinkers such as Frantz Fanon (1925–1961) gained ground and offered a rationale for moving beyond theistic formulations of the social world and related strategies for negotiating it. Through this turn to revolutionary thought, the importance of the church in particular and theism in general was questioned, and other modes for securing life-meaning were advanced. Such a shift wasn't always a quiet turn but, rather, a vocal critique of theism for its participation in the oppression of the marginalized. Its moral and ethical commitments were challenged aggressively and found wanting in that they were seen to be in line with the status quo, with the thinking of oppressors. The Black Church became, in light of this critique, another tool for subduing the oppressed: pacifying and distracting them with talk of heaven as opposed to social transformation and ecopolitical revolution. Where's the freedom in aping white normativity as a way to advance Black people—all justified through a convenient theology of inclusion? This shift in orientation meant more than a decade of Black life that didn't require attention to major theistic traditions, and, even when spirituality remained an important source of meaning-making, there were African-based and more humanism-friendly orientations such as voodoo and Lucumi that offered a form of spiritual commitment that embraced materiality and denounced some of the more body-disregarding practices of Black churches. The Christian faith's control over the language of life-meaning was showing cracks and vulnerabilities.

While the role of the Black Church remained a topic of conversation and an assumption for many, the decades after the civil rights movement marked a period when Black Americans could explore sources for and naming(s) of life-meaning using a more secular vocabulary and grammar. This isn't to say that this secularity—and, in many cases, a humanist posture—wasn't met with suspicion when expressed. Again, as the comments of Oprah Winfrey and Steve Harvey might suggest, it could entail rejection by friends or family members who believed anything other than a traditional theistic position was unacceptable: "How can you be moral and a good person if you don't believe in God? If you don't have the Bible and the example of Jesus to follow? Aren't you afraid of going to hell—and that's where you'll go if you don't get your life right!" Such pronouncements were often followed by a request to pray for the sinner, although condemnation was really a needed affirmation of the Christian's theology and faith. They couldn't both be right, so the sinner's failure would be a sign of the Christian's rightness. Any example of failure, of trouble, any indicator that the heathen's life wasn't on track, was viewed as a sign that God punishes sinners and rewards the righteous. And, even though the latter may have to stretch to try to find signs of rewards in a context of ongoing misery, there's always redemptive suffering to fall back on. Despite its efforts to demonize the godless, the Black Church could not retain its dominance. Greater public expression of nontheistic points of view meant it became easier to hold such positions: one was no longer the only humanist, the only freethinker, the only agnostic, the only skeptic. This sense of "others" provided a bit of relief and shelter within a social context still marked by some assumptions of theism, despite church decline. Those suspicious of theistic claims, and those more decidedly opposed to them, had time to regroup and could consider Black humanism, which was becoming increasingly visible. This matters because the Black community had been overdetermined by theism. Thus, the increase in the number of Black Americans who have broken with this social conditioning and denounced various modes of theism as having no particular value for them is important.

In 2011, atheist activist Mark D. Hatcher asked what some have wondered for decades: "Would the civil rights movement have been necessary without Christianity?"[5] This places center stage the manner in which theism has marginalized and dehumanized anyone not of "*the* faith" through an insider and outsider posture. "We mustn't forget," he went on, "that the movement came on the heels of the Harlem Renaissance, an era of enlightenment and critical thinking that was rife with atheists and agnostics; nor should we forget that plenty of open atheists, such as A. Philip Randolph, played integral parts in the civil rights movement."[6] Regardless of such biting critiques over the years, the Black Church wouldn't give up that easily. Its theological justification and ethical sensibilities were showing internal problems and inconsistencies, but the ritual structures maintained a vibrancy that would motivate many, even when the thought and rhetoric accompanying the rituals fell short. There was always the reluctance of the United States to actually transform itself in line with its civil rights promises and democratic possibilities. Black Americans would always need an outlet, a way of forging a sense of self in relationship to something grander and more stable. For some, theism, particularly in the form of the Black Church, was still a good place to look. Wearing their Sunday best, they walked into sanctuaries. . . .

The "me-centered" 1980s left some Blacks feeling empty and in need of connections to something—some community, some rituals, some practices that involved more than radical individualism in a land in which Black subjectivity was still an open question. For a decade after the civil rights struggle, the Black middle class played by the rules, went to the right (read white) schools, lived in the right neighborhoods, joined the acceptable clubs, secured the jobs needed in order to advance, and so on, but racism still served as a powerful barrier to full participation in the life of the nation. That is to say, life-meaning writ large was still informed and influenced by the dehumanizing structures of white supremacy and white privilege. Many went back to Black churches and other Black theistic organizations to address a sense of social and cultural loss—to reconnect to the history and content of Black culture, so much of which they'd sacrificed in order to fit in to the dominant culture. For some, the Black Church provided a way to think and be "Black" in a context in which, despite the civil rights movement, race mattered and could be deadly. Some returned to Black Christian denominations, while others embraced a range of theistic traditions (African-based traditions or Sunni Islam, which claims roughly three million African Americans). This tells us little, however, concerning the nature or depth of their theological commitments. There's no reason to assume that all those who returned to the church, for example, held to the assumed faith commitments; instead, we should think in terms of a diversity of reasons for being a member. Reasons for church membership could range from social networking and cultural connection to a hardcore conviction regarding the need for heavenly salvation. Few churches would check commitment, although a "soft" form of verification might involve Pentecostal churches that anticipated growth in spiritual power attested to through gifts of the Holy Spirit such as speaking in tongues. Yet, in most cases, attendance, perhaps even some level of service and tithing (giving 10 percent of one's income) would be a baseline, which doesn't entail an expressed theological position. Hence, atheists, humanists, and other nontheists could embrace and enjoy the ritualized fellowship and connection to other Black Americans, as long as they could tolerate the theological assumptions embedded in sermons and endure the occasional call for acts of faith. In exchange for the sociocultural (and potentially economic) benefits, the more theologically forceful dimensions of church life might be a small price to pay. This sentiment is reflected in the words of Hatcher, when he says,

> While white cultures had 4-H clubs, country clubs, access to mental-health care and political rallies, the blacks with no access to these things due to segregation found it under the steeple. These powerful roots make it hard to extinguish associations with religion, even among the doubters.[7]

Nontheists in Black theistic organizations (primarily Black churches) would need to maintain a type of "Don't ask, don't tell" policy. This would be easier with churches more progressive in their policies and less literal in their biblical interpretation and doctrinal claims, but nontheists would have little difficulty deciphering types of churches and selecting accordingly. What they didn't gain from church involvement could be supplemented through participation in secular organizations and fellowships, such as fraternities and sororities. In short, some Black humanists hid out in Black churches, keeping their questions to themselves, selectively participating, and getting what they could without sacrificing all their principles. There was a tradeoff that they maneuvered with great care.

Nevertheless, church came with a cost that often necessitated that Black nontheists compartmentalize their identities and lives. As Liz Ross reflects, "I realized that the church itself was not a space that helped me empower myself, particularly as a Black woman and someone in the LGBTQ community."[8] The same folks who claimed the radical love of God for all found it easy to condemn and damage those who didn't fit their particular sense of righteousness. As Asher_Jak put it,

> The more I thought about it, the more I felt I couldn't trust that I was following the word of God and not the word of Matthew or Mark. I didn't feel sure of what the right interpretation was because I heard so many conflicting things from other Christians. The more questions I asked, the less

I could hang with the answers given to me. It was pretty clear that Christianity, as I understood it, wasn't my thing.[9]

Disdain for nontheistic positions displayed by some Black Americans within churches and other theistic organizations suggests a moral and ethical quagmire. Novelist Wrath James White captures the inconsistency: "In most African American communities, it is more acceptable to be a criminal who goes to church on Sunday, while selling drugs to kids all week, than to be an atheist who . . . contributes to society and supports his family."[10] Still, as Bey rightly remarks, the growth in the number of Black Americans who hold no particular religious affiliation, and who chafe at assumptions like these, has meaning: "There are a whole lot of us who are not going to nod and amen our way through things. So many of us are putting an end to that unfortunate practice. Everyone's soon going to know us."[11]

RISE OF THE BLACK NONES

The twenty-first century marked a significant uptick in the percentage of Black Americans who claim no particular religious affiliation: the nones. This growth is part of a national trend. A recent Gallup Poll indicates the percentage of US citizens claiming belief in god(s) has dropped: 98 percent of those polled in the 1960s claimed belief, while the same question asked between 2014 and 2017 showed an affirmative response of only 81 percent. This is matched by a significant decrease in church attendance and membership. A Pew Research Center study intensifies the situation by claiming that "about three-in-ten US adults are now religiously unaffiliated." Does this mean they are actual atheists? Not exactly, but it does indicate that working through life issues doesn't require processes offered by traditional theistic communities.[12] According to the Pew Research Center's study, the percentage of Black Americans who rely on the Church—if one measures this by regular attendance—has also decreased. Regardless of whether or not churches acknowledge this publicly, it has become increasingly difficult to ignore, particularly in terms of younger groupings of Blacks. The numbers indicate a growing percentage of Black Americans moving away from theism.

The most significant indicator of decline in the centrality of theism for Black Americans is this: the percentage of US adults who "describe their religion as 'nothing in particular' has increased over the last two decades—from roughly 12% in 2007 to 20% in 2021. And there is a noteworthy trend with respect to Black Americans—particularly those between the ages of 18–49."[13] Relatedly, according to Pew, "overall, 'nones' make up 21% of Black U. S. adults. Most in that category say their religion is 'nothing in particular' (18%), while far fewer describe themselves as agnostic (2%) or atheist (1%)."[14] These statistics don't justify making a large claim concerning any particular mode of disbelief; many Black nones "believe in some sort of organizing power," although they don't necessarily describe that power as "God." But what it does suggest is a shift concerning the practice of certain forms of theism, and the speed with which this is happening deserves attention. As one article notes, "Over more than a decade, the share of Black Americans who say that they have no religious affiliation has risen more dramatically than whites, Hispanics, or Asians."[15] More to the point, "among African Americans, the increase in the share of the 'nones' was much larger, more than 15 percentage points. In 2008, African Americans were the least likely to be 'nones' (19.5%), but by 2020 they were more likely to say that they had no religious affiliation than white or Hispanic respondents (34.9%)."[16] This development should get us thinking not that Blacks are leaving *all* forms of religion, but that there is greater diversity concerning how religion is understood, described, and practiced by Black Americans—and this, of course, includes Black humanism.

Some of these Black nones left theistic organizations and now publicly disassociate themselves from those systems of belief. For example, Liz Ross has had this to say:

> I came to identify as an atheist after exploring the question of why there is so much senseless suffering, and recognizing ways in which white supremacy, patriarchy, and anti-LGBTQ sentiment is embedded in religious doctrine

and in our culture. The experience also played a pivotal role in liberating my mind from negative self-reflection. The god that I was brought up to worship was not a reflection of myself. Nor did the tenets of his followers' holy book, and the society in which I was raised, offer me support to fully recognize my dignity as Black, female, and not heterosexual.[17]

Leaving theism can be a painful experience, involving some of the isolation and animosity that humanists hiding out in Black churches seek to avoid. A *Washington Post* story on African Americans who are nontheists highlights this challenge in relationship to Alix Jules. "Now, at age 37," the reporter writes, "Jules has been ostracized by his mother and cousins. His story is typical of many African-American atheists who say that to 'come out' as nonbelievers in their community is to risk everything—friends, family, business ties, even their racial and cultural identity."[18] Others avoid this trauma because they were never part of a theistic community. This doesn't necessarily preclude a backlash, as activist and organizer Mandisa Thomas notes: "Though I was raised secular—a rarity in my community—I've had to endure ostracism from family and friends as a result of openly identifying as an atheist. However," and this is key,

my journey is far from tragic. In founding my organization, Black Nonbelievers, in 2011, I have been fortunate to connect with others who were either raised secular like myself, or who were brought up extremely religious and left it behind. And they have done so bravely, defying the perception and expectation that all blacks blindly accept religion.[19]

For some nones, part of their assertion of self—the expression of their identity—involves strong and open critique of theism(s). For others, there is a sense that theistic belief isn't a group issue, so to speak, but should be left to individuals to address. The presence of these two postures, among others, can result in some conflict, as Sydney (no surname given) relates when talking about dating as a nontheist:

> I also have trouble dating other atheists because they want to actively bash Christianity and other religions and come from a morally superior background. Personally, I don't have a problem with religions, Christianity or otherwise. I see how they can be empowering for others even if they don't do anything for me, so conversations where people talked down on religious people make me very uncomfortable.[20]

In a similar vein, Darrin Johnson remarks: "My atheism is not a thing of 'I know better than you and so I'm better than you.' I love my people be they religious or not . . . I'd rather work with a Black religious person working for Black liberation, than a Black atheist who's in it for social climbing."[21]

With this public presence of Black nontheism came an uptick in the number of organizations available to them. For example, the Black Skeptics Los Angeles organization founded by Sikivu Hutchinson offers a type of third space (over against home and work) for nonbelievers: "The group started by simply offering space for Black and secular people of color to meet and later expanded to resources for nonbelievers. It now offers scholarships for graduating seniors and aid for secular people of color—especially during COVID-19."[22] What Black Skeptics and other groups like it offer is a "soft place to land" for those who don't fit into theistic communities and who have felt marginalized within predominately white nontheistic circles, where their social concerns often take a back seat to issues of science education and separation of church and state. This alternate space is a major concern for US-based Black nontheistic organizations and gatherings, but it isn't restricted to the US context, as the challenges of Blackness in relationship to humanism isn't limited to any particular nation–state. One need only think, for instance, of the Association of Black Humanists in the United Kingdom, which, according to Audrey Simmons, seeks to

> give people space to talk. People need to vent, be heard, or
> have their experiences acknowledged. Also, they're usually

looking for information and knowledge. We have a range
of topics we cover . . . Sometimes they come for one session
because they have a question, or to work out where they
are on their journey . . . We have people who still go to
church who come to us.[23]

What one gathers from the claims and commitments
expressed within these Black nontheistic, often humanistic-
oriented communities, is preoccupation with issues of justice
(as both a personal and communal concern) as a dimension
of a nontheistic self-understanding. One gets a sense of this
expansive function for nontheism in the personal reflection
of Asher_Jak:

I was looking for a belief system that would allow me to
be a good person but not necessarily believe in God, and
at that point, I realized, I might as well just be an atheist
who focuses on doing good. So, I started reading more
in-depth about social justice issues . . . I'm trying to make
the world a better place. I just don't need spirituality or the
supernatural for that to happen."[24]

Or, as author and organizer Candace Gorham notes,

As a secular Black female, it's impossible for me not to work
toward the betterment of my community. We take care of

those around us, Black women; that's what we do. Once I separated from religion and fully embraced the humanist ideal that people must take care of each other because we're all we have, the urge to engage in social justice activism became too strong to ignore.[25]

▲ ▲ ▲ ▲ ▲ ▲ ▲ ▲ ▲ ▲

CHAPTER 4

BLACK HUMANISM AND JUSTICE WORK

We are the ones that change the world. In recognizing that this responsibility is ours, not gods, people begin to feel more accountable for effecting positive change in the world around us.

—DIA BROWN

The work of Black humanism as a mechanism for meaning-making doesn't hold to the same theological assumptions that animate, for example, Black churches. But it does share with many of these churches an ethics of engagement that fosters a desire to spread the word concerning the benefits of their (non)belief system. As historian Christopher Cameron notes, "New black atheists are not content to personally reject religion but instead have a goal of spreading freethought to the broader black community."[1]

ACTIVISM: NINETEENTH AND TWENTIETH CENTURIES

The subject of religion and activism often calls to mind the presence of church leaders and church laity in civil rights protests during the twentieth century, or even early in the political efforts of Black church figures such as Ida B. Wells-Barnett (1862–1931) and her struggle against racial violence in the form of lynching, or Bishop Henry McNeal Turner (1834–1915) and his protest against racial discrimination through religiously fueled back-to-Africa activism. For such figures, belief in God and God's will with respect to Black people motivated struggle against racial violence in an effort to establish new social relationships more in line with the coming "kingdom of God."

There is ample evidence of a similar commitment to activism on the part of those claiming no real ties to theism. Think of Frederick Douglass (1819–1895), who argued that he didn't know the value of prayer until he prayed with his legs—which is to indicate his reliance on human power and practice rather than calling on some sort of divine assistance. Despite ongoing discussion regarding Douglass's commitments, I would argue that there is enough evidence to suggest nontheistic sensibilities. It is true that Douglass, like W. E. B. Du Bois after him, was a bit guarded in terms of public expression of such delicate opinions, but his actions and his thinking as recorded in speeches and his autobiographies suggest a posture toward the world not unlike Black humanism. At the very least, Douglass understood his beliefs to be out of line with dominant perspectives and liable to result in negative response. Regarding this veiled sense of difference, he writes in a letter: "I have no doubt that the avowal of my liberal opinions will drive many from me who were once my friends and even exclude me from many platforms upon which I was a welcome speaker, but such is the penalty which every man must suffer who admits a new truth into his mind."[2] While his language is a bit coded, Douglass scholar William L. Van Deburg makes clear Douglass's rejection of the idea of God (as a distinct and "super" being) and his dependence on humans to make a difference in the world. In supporting this claim, Van Deburg references a speech given by Douglass as part of the American Anti-Slavery Society Convention in 1870: "I like to thank men . . . I want to express my love to God and gratitude to God, by thanking those faithful men and women, who have devoted the great energies of their soul to the welfare of mankind. It is only through such men and such women that I can get a glimpse of God anywhere."[3] What one finds here is not a denial of human effort for the sake of some cosmic force but, rather, a full reliance on what humans' work seeks to achieve.

In thinking about W. E. B. Du Bois (1868–1963), his attention to the potential of the Black Church for material transformation of life circumstances, and his writings on theistic religion do not mean that he himself was a theist. In fact, there is much to suggest otherwise. Du Bois was something of a freethinker, committed to reason and logical inquiry. He spoke of a sense of wonder and awe of life that was framed by human creativity and ingenuity. Even his collection *Prayers for Dark People* (1909–10) seems an ode to a cultural form of expression, similar to what one would later gain with nonbeliever James Weldon Johnson's presentation of the Black sermonic tradition in *God's Trombones* (1927). Du Bois is also the man who, when asked to lead prayer at Wilberforce University, refused the invitation. God, if one follows Du Bois's full line of reasoning, isn't the biblical figure, nor the figure of the Black Church tradition, but a way of naming a unity of expression—a gathering of human determination and potentiality within a common frame of reference. According to his own words, he was a freethinker, and, as such, Du Bois associated the greatness of the physical universe with the grand unity.[4] Hence, his activism doesn't draw on theologically derived claims of teleological sensibilities that see a divine purpose in human actions; rather, his undeniable sense of activism did not extend beyond what human minds could conceive and human hands produce.

Mention has already been made of Black communists during the early twentieth century. Related to this—and although he would later disavow any claims that he was an atheist—Langston Hughes (1901–1967) wrote poems such as the communistically inclined "Goodbye Christ" (1932) that urged a turn away from Christian faith to the grounded work of human hands. Hughes called for Jesus to move along because his replacements had arrived (Mao and others), and they were better equipped to meet the needs of the suffering masses.

A similar economic model and radical sensibility are housed also in the activism of the Black Power movement in general and the Black Panther Party (BPP) in particular. This isn't to say these activists didn't interact with churches; it is important to recognize they aligned themselves with the resource these churches represented—namely, meeting spaces and effective methods of communicating information quickly. To some extent, the Black Power movement was opposed to the theologically driven approach of the dominant civil rights movement. Appeals to God and redemptive suffering models weren't attractive, as Black Power advocates believed that a country that operates inconsistently with its theistic claims can't be approached and sufficiently changed through appeals to theism. More to the point, there was no evidence that such appeals were grounded in anything more than a wish. Instead of reliance on a God concept and a church tied to that concept, it was better to raise the consciousness of the community. As Huey P. Newton (1942–1989), a founding figure in the BPP, notes,

> After a short harmonious relationship with the church, in fact a very good relationship, we were divorced from the church, and shortly after that found ourselves out of favor with the whole Black community. We found ourselves in somewhat of a void alienated from the whole community. We had no way of being effective as far as developing the community was concerned. The only way we could aid in that process of revolution—and revolution is a process rather than conclusion or a set of principles, or any particular action—was by raising the consciousness of the community.[5]

How does raising the consciousness of the community take place? In part, as Newton demonstrates, it involves a philosophical shift made possible through scientific knowledge. For example, Newton argued that God was a way of naming ignorance, a lack of information, but adherence to the concept of God would decrease as human knowledge increased. Tied to self-defense, this new way of thinking could ground transformative activism within Black communities because, "as man becomes freer he knows more about the universe, he tends to control more and he therefore gains more control over himself. That is what freedom is all about."[6] Various proponents of the Black Power movement sought to counter white aggression with a call for Black self-determination, which would serve to foster a sense of humanity and personhood, not through an appeal to theological anthropology—that humans are created in the image of God—but through recognition of Black people as subjects in history.

Human accountability and responsibility were used to forge a sense of ethical obligation that gave no consideration to cosmic forces laboring on behalf of humans. At best, claims concerning the existence and presence of a God involved in human affairs were met with suspicion and, in many cases, with energetic denunciation. Turning again to Newton, one finds this thinking on the party's "divorce" from the Black Church:

> As far as the church was concerned, the Black Panther Party and other community groups emphasized the political and criticized the spiritual. We said the church is only a ritual, it is irrelevant, and therefore we will have nothing to do with it . . . Once we stepped outside of the church with that criticism, we stepped outside of the whole thing that the community was involved in and we said, "You follow your example; your reality is not true and you don't need it."[7]

In making this claim, Newton isn't dismissing the need of Black people to resolve life issues, to find life-meaning. Instead, he is pointing out the failure of theism to offer that meaning in a way that safeguards the integrity of Black life. The ten points defining the BPP's platform help secure this integrity:

1. We want freedom. We want power to determine the destiny of our Black Community.
2. We want full employment for our people.
3. We want an end to the robbery by the Capitalists of our Black Community.
4. We want decent housing, fit for shelter of human beings.
5. We want education for our people that exposes the true nature of this decadent American society. We want education that teaches us our true history and our role in the present-day society.
6. We want all Black men to be exempt from military service.
7. We want an immediate end to police brutality and murder of Black people.
8. We want freedom for all Black men held in federal, state, county and city prisons and jails.
9. We want all Black people when brought to trial to be tried in court by a jury of their peer group or

> people from their Black Communities, as defined
> by the Constitution of the United States.
> 10. We want land, bread, housing, education, clothing,
> justice and peace.[8]

Anger couldn't be appeased through promises of peace and prosperity induced by attention to sacred texts inspired by nonhuman forces. Needed was revolution—"Power to the People!"—because a radical break had to be made with the existing socioeconomic structures that reduced human meaning and importance and supported inequality. Gaining some inspiration from secular thinkers such as Frantz Fanon, through his books *The Wretched of the Earth* (1961) and *Black Skin, White Masks* (1952), as well as from the godless push for communal advancement reflected in Chairman Mao's *Red Book*, they worked to break free of a theological monopoly on activism that failed to recognize how empire-inspired and colonialism-inflected Christianity advanced the interests of the few. The BPP held to a different set of sacred texts—books that grounded life in the stuff of the world. The natural, historically situated, and materially known circumstances of life could only be addressed through human effort, which is all that is real. Black Power and its champions sought the fostering of life-meaning within the confines of human history, premised strictly on the efforts of human hands, hearts, and minds. In addition to challenging the socioeconomic and political markers of white supremacy, this move required freeing Black minds and hearts from what individuals like Douglass called "internalized racism." This had to involve a challenge to Black theism, as well as its advocates and its various organizations.

One shouldn't think a humanistic presence within the twentieth-century civil rights struggle was limited to Black Power movement figures or more marginal strategic communities. While the dominant narrative downplays them, Black nontheists were central to the more widely recognized civil rights movement, influencing and informing strategy and talking points. Bayard Rustin (1912–1987), for example, played a major role in developing the nature and expression of the movement's take on nonviolent direct action. A. Philip Randolph's (1899–1979) labor organizing extended the reach of the movement and served as the framework for the March on Washington for Jobs and Justice in 1963. Furthermore, Black nontheists like James Forman (1928–2005) played a key role in the Student Nonviolent Coordinating Committee (SNCC), and they did so in light of a belief in human responsibility and disbelief in the idea of a God involved in human affairs. As Forman wrote,

The belief in a supreme being or God weakens the will of a people to change conditions themselves. As a Negro who has grown up in the United States, I believe that the belief in God has hurt my people. We have put off doing something about our condition on this earth because we have believed that God was going to take care of business in heaven.[9]

This thinking extended beyond his work with SNCC and took vibrant expression in his announcement of the Black Manifesto (1969) at Riverside Church in New York City. This manifesto highlights the role played by theistic organizations in anti-Black racism and demanded the release of millions of dollars and other resources to address their wrongdoing and make amends. Forman announced from the floor of the church:

> We are therefore demanding of the white Christian churches and Jewish synagogues which are part and parcel of the system of capitalism, that they begin to pay reparations to black people in this country. We are demanding $500,000,000 from the Christian white churches and the Jewish synagogues. This total comes to 15 dollars per nigger. This is a low estimate for we maintain there are probably more than 30,000,000 black people in this country. $15 a nigger is not a large sum of money and we know that the churches and synagogues have a tremendous wealth and its membership, white America, has profited and still exploits black people. We are also not unaware that the exploitation of colored peoples around the world is aided and abetted by the white Christian churches and synagogues. This demand for $500,000,000 is not an idle resolution or empty

words. Fifteen dollars for every black brother and sister in the United States is only a beginning of the reparations due us as people who have been exploited and degraded, brutalized, killed and persecuted. Underneath all of this exploitation, the racism of this country has produced a psychological effect upon us that we are beginning to shake off. We are no longer afraid to demand our full rights as a people in this decadent society.[10]

While involvement of these key figures and countless others didn't change the perception of the civil rights movement as a God-driven project, their efforts do provide an opportunity to better understand the place and practice of Black humanism as a guiding force for societal transformation. In this arrangement, the future isn't guaranteed through cosmic intervention but through the possibility of improvement by human, intentional activism.

ACTIVISM: TWENTY-FIRST CENTURY

During the late twentieth and early twenty-first centuries, nontheistic modes of expression—atheism in particular— gained increased public attention through writers such as Richard Dawkins and Christopher Hitchens, who criticized and mocked Christianity and Islam. They called for the dominance of a science- and reason-based philosophy of life in place of these long-standing theistic traditions. These New

Atheist preachers, so to speak, captured the imagination of an international audience, including some Black Americans. However, their failure to address issues of racial justice limited their reach into Black communities: disbelief didn't free Black people from racism and an obligation to produce social change. In fact, for some white and Black nontheists, New Atheism, particularly online, was much too close to the alt-right in its thinking. As Chris Stedman, a white humanist activist in Minnesota, wrote in 2018:

> I'm still an activist, but after nearly a decade of active participation in online atheism (a loose community of forums, blogs, YouTube channels, and fandoms of figures like evolutionary biologist Richard Dawkins and writer Sam Harris), I mostly stepped away from the online side of atheism a few years ago. One of the biggest reasons for this was my growing concern over its failure to adequately address some of its darker currents—such as overt sexism, racism, and anti-Muslim bias.[11]

Black nontheist and activist Sincere Kirabo puts a fine point on the issue of the New Atheism when turning to one of the "four horsemen" of the movement—Sam Harris.

> Harris's denigration of identity politics screams positionality bias, where any position or movement that deviates from widely accepted thought and practice are pejoratively

labelled "identity politics." At the same time, dialogue, systems, and political engagement that favor the interests of cisgender, heterosexual white male mainstream narratives tend to be exempt from such uncharitable critique.[12]

Kirabo's article points to the manner in which Black non-theists began critiquing the underlying white privilege of the New Atheism and looked for alternatives that embraced a way of life both beyond the confinement of assumed white privilege and white supremacy, and beyond the assumption that reason and science were outside the reach of social prejudice. In fact, in numerous instances, the effort of some nontheists to include issues of justice in the atheist movement was met with scorn and derision.

The meaning of life offered by New Atheism wasn't meaning-*full* enough for many Black Americans seeking to make their humanism an outlet for social engagement. Yet, as Kirabo makes clear:

Of course, opposing a deluge of anti-black contempt will produce passion—the only people not passionate about fighting for freedom from misrepresentation and oppression are the oblivious, the deceased, or those unaffected by said social imbalance. As long as deprivations courtesy of racism and white supremacy continue to adversely impact the life circumstances of Black America, expect those in touch with this reality to confront injustice with all the rage, frustration, and anxiety to be expected from enduring life in a land where your very humanity is questioned, disregarded, and despised.[13]

The stakes remain high for Black American humanists, who are continuously reminded that they live in a country that despises them for their Blackness, as well as for their disbelief. For Black women, this jeopardy is extended to include gender bias. And for those who claim a sexuality outside the traditional male-female dichotomy, there is yet another source of disregard with which to contend. Knowing this, Black American practitioners of humanism spent much of the end of the twentieth century and the beginning of the twenty-first century looking for a way to break through this uncomfortable and deadly dilemma. The time is now, as Lydia Mason makes so very clear. "There came a day," she writes,

when I got tired of waiting for a god to fix the world for me. I realized that I had the ability to set my own standards for the kind of person I wanted to be, and that I had the responsibility for upholding those standards. As I entered high school, I embraced humanism wholeheartedly, and began fighting for justice for all people on the basis of race, gender, sexual orientation and disability. I decided to stop waiting for someone or something to change the world, and instead be that change myself.[14]

Dia Brown adds to this sense of human accountability as a dimension of nontheism when saying, "We are the ones that change the world. In recognizing that this responsibility is ours, not gods, people begin to feel more accountable for effecting positive change in the world around us."[15]

For much of the first decade of this century, there was little reason to believe that a nontheistic sensibility would be welcomed in the arena of public engagement. However, for a complex community of Black humanists, the election of President Barack Obama signaled new possibilities, a new United States open to all. In his 2009 inaugural address, Obama included both believers and nonbelievers as rightful holders of the promise and obligations of the United States. The actual statement is important here:

> We will not apologize for our way of life, nor will we waver in its defense. And for those who seek to advance their aims by inducing terror and slaughtering innocents, we say to you now that our spirit is stronger and cannot be broken—you cannot outlast us, and we will defeat you.
>
> For we know that our patchwork heritage is a strength, not a weakness. We are a nation of Christians and Muslims, Jews and Hindus, and nonbelievers.[16]

It is one word—"nonbelievers"—but it names a category of US residents normally excluded and held with deep suspicion. This disbelief, this nontheism, isn't presented here as a problem to solve but as an important component of US identity: it represents one of the frameworks of thought that enables the type of hard work necessary to transform the nation in light of the sense of profound possibility that gained him the White House. No other president had ever included nontheists in the roll call of productive and protected US citizens. What's more, I can think of no other contemporary president whose vision of the US citizenry and of justice work within a country determined to be the best version of itself captured the imagination of theists and nontheists alike. Humanists claimed Obama as one of their own, as did theists. His rhetoric and social sensibilities spoke to democratic possibility across religious positions. Although he is a Christian, he spoke of the United States in a way that reminded people of their shared humanity. Obama's sense of hope and the way in which he articulated what that hope might produce lacked a decidedly Christian undertone; it was inclusive in its reach. While just a single line in his speech—"We are a nation of Christians and Muslims, Jews and Hindus, and nonbelievers"—it represented for Black humanists a turn, which blended two concerns and the culmination of much effort: a Black president marked the fulfillment of a long-held goal, and a president who acknowledged their presence was more than most could have anticipated. He did not privilege, like all before him, the Christian faith but instead extended the range of meaning-making processes—or religion—in the United States along a spectrum of approaches, all valid, all valuable. (The speech did nevertheless conclude with the traditional invocation "God bless America.")

This call for inclusiveness wouldn't come without its challenges. It's important to keep in mind that the years of the Obama presidency were marked by hate crimes, by the murder of Blacks in public spaces and church sanctuaries. In too many of these cases—in fact, most of these cases—the killing of Blacks was met with limited legal consequences. This wasn't new. Extralegal lynchings during the period of Jim and Jane Crow, after Reconstruction and through the civil rights movement, were frequently public events conducted with perpetrators receiving little in the way of formal punishment. Because it was assumed that Blacks need not be appreciated or valued, they weren't protected by the rule of law. Still, law enforcement officials murdering Blacks who didn't appear to be guilty of anything other than being Black in public seems even more grievous in the post–civil rights era. Black children murdered for being out of place, while walking back home from the store, playing in a park—or just being. Such injustice spawned the development of a new movement: Black Lives Matter (BLM).

Often labeled "not your grandmother's civil rights movement," BLM was initiated as a social "love letter" to Black America. It became a mechanism for activism in the wake of the police murder of Michael Brown in 2014, and it grew to include a range of concerns that spoke to the complexity of the Black community. This is to say that "Black Lives Matter is an ideological and political intervention in a world where Black lives are systematically and intentionally targeted for demise. It is an affirmation of Black folks' humanity, our contributions to this society, and our resilience in the face of deadly oppression."[17] Something of this sentiment is found in the words of Bridgett Crutchfield, a humanist activist, when describing herself and her responsibilities:

> being empathetic, giving a damn, hurts. I care about the people in the communities I belong to. Walking away, as inviting as that sounds, isn't an option. I won't give up, but I'm at ease knowing my voice is one of many—a harmonious choir that sings songs of spirit, war, equality, and justice—raising one fist as the other wraps around a plow.[18]

BLM's objectives support a broad sense of abolition, and they don't claim any particular moral or ethical framework. Nor do they assume a Christian interpretation of moral value, or an Islamic interpretation, or any particular sectarian reading. Instead, the seven demands involve attention to the basic social structure of collective life that hampers a vast sense of well-being:

1. Convict and ban Trump from future political office;
2. Expel Republican members of Congress who attempted to overturn the election and incited a white supremacist attack;
3. Launch a full investigation into the ties between white supremacy and the Capitol Police, law enforcement, and the military;
4. Permanently ban Trump from all digital media platforms;
5. Defund the police;
6. Don't let the coup be used as an excuse to crack down on our movement;
7. Pass the BREATHE act.[19]

Started by three Black women—Alicia Garza, Patrisse Cullors, and Opal Tometi—and representing the complexity and layered nature of life and relationships within Black American communities, BLM grew to become both an online and physical movement concerning the possibility of a new social world inclusive of the most marginalized. It reflects an alternate organizational model that pushed against the hierarchical structure of the twentieth-century civil rights movement—no single leader, but, rather, a sense that BLM is a leader-*full* praxis of protest. Related to this, BLM does not assume the authority of Black preachers, as the civil rights movement had; in fact, it does not assume Christianity in particular, or theism in general, to be the guiding philosophy of life animating the movement. Instead, it is structured in such a way as to make Black humanists feel as included and as comfortable as Black theists. As author and organizer Norm Allen states, "Progressive humanism and the Black Lives Matter movement make for a good match. Rather than blindly defend the powers that be, we must continue to hold their feet to the fire and demand what we deserve."[20] But why? What fosters this good match?

The match isn't without its tensions and points of disagreement. However, Kirabo seems to offer a response, even if not directly, to this question when highlighting the compatibility of humanist principles with BLM aims and strategies. Both, for instance, hold to the notion of human connection across difference, and the call for the well-being of all is consistent with a humanist attention to "coexistence marked by equitable rapport and reciprocity," to "unfettered, egalitarian human welfare," to a "humane society."[21] As many Black humanists note, what one gains through attention to BLM is opportunity for "a more intersectional and more politicized scope of activism through encouraging social justice competency within secular spaces as well as by engaging in racial, gender, and restorative justice activism."[22] Much of this points to recognition that BLM doesn't demand a theistic motivation or source for involvement. Instead, to the extent it sees that human accountability and possibility as motivation for action, it is open to a significant range of religious perspectives, because the one thing all religions have in common is people. As Melynda Price puts it:

> The #BlackLivesMatter movement is noteworthy because it has intentionally positioned itself outside of black religious institutions while also utilizing religious spaces, people, and ideologies as part of its transformative work. The rhetoric is not saturated in the Christian tradition of the 1960s civil rights movement, but it is clear they have their eyes on the prize . . . Religion has long been part of the moral refashioning that African Americans have engaged in as part of their efforts to render themselves cognizable legal and political subjects. Where #BlackLivesMatter may be distinct is in their challenge to the idea that the cloak of religion . . . has ever been an effective tool in making black lives matter.[23]

This is not to say that BLM is intrinsically humanistic but, rather, that its self-understanding, its philosophy of engagement, and its sense of community allow for Black humanists to comfortably claim participation—to feel included and

appreciated in their humanism, not in spite of their humanism. The language of spirituality does exist within BLM as
in, for instance, Cullors's statement that "the fight to save our
life is a spiritual fight."[24] Many Black nonbelievers might veer
away from the language of spirituality, associating it with the
churches they left behind. Nothing about BLM as a loose
configuration of organizations requires a particular theistic
understanding of this phrase, however. This sense of deep
entanglement isn't the sole domain of any particular tradition;
instead, BLM leaves it to participants to determine the best
way to name and harness the nature of "spiritual fight." Keep
in mind how spiritual principles are defined here: "The movement is committed to spiritual principles, such as 'healing
justice'—which uses a range of holistic approaches to address
trauma and oppression by centering emotional and spiritual
well-being—and 'transformative justice' which assist with
creating processes to repair harm without violence."[25] The
vocabulary used in BLM speaks to the vitality of shared humanity and privileges, and it relies on a grammar of inclusion
allowing for continued evolution of social concern(s). While
it might share some similarities with more progressive Black
churches, the reasoning for BLM's expansive sense of care
isn't grounded in what a divine figure says one should do, but
in what reflection on life within the context of human history
makes evident. Only principles that advance an agenda of
justice are maintained, and experience is the final litmus test

of importance and meaning. Hence, BLM is able to embrace populations that Black churches tend to despise. One could reasonably argue that BLM as a mass movement for justice has provided more opportunities for inclusion across belief systems without erasing differences.

We get a sense of this more expansive, less theologically driven grammar for activism in the framing of the movement. There is a sense of solidarity surpassing that typically highlighted in terms of the early civil rights movement and the leadership model of most Black theistic organizations:

> As organizers who work with everyday people, BLM members see and understand significant gaps in movement spaces and leadership. Black liberation movements in this country have created room, space, and leadership mostly for Black heterosexual, cisgender men—leaving women, queer and transgender people, and others either out of the movement or in the background to move the work forward with little or no recognition. As a network, we have always recognized the need to center the leadership of women and queer and trans people. To maximize our movement muscle, and to be intentional about not replicating harmful practices that excluded so many in past movements for liberation, we made a commitment to placing those at the margins closer to the center.[26]

In addition, unlike the civil rights movement's outcome-driven strategy, which assumes that because God works with humans, freedom will result, BLM seems to operate based on a sense of perpetual struggle, which is a more humanistic understanding of the promise and pitfalls of human engagement with the world.

CHAPTER 5

▲ ▲ ▲ ▲ ▲ ▲ ▲ ▲ ▲ ▲

BLACK HUMANISTS IN COMMUNITY

For me and other Black nonbelievers like me, it's about turning Humanism from something we read about in books, into something that we do together.

—ALIX JULES

B lack humanism can be practiced within the comfort of one's home. It doesn't require involvement with a larger community. However, for some Black humanists, participation in a larger community is both a comfort and an opportunity to be affirmed. For some Black humanists, belonging to a community affords joy and a deep sense of connection that can't be duplicated through reading, thinking, and being a humanist alone.

COMMUNITY WITH UNITARIANS

During the early twentieth century, some Black Americans nurtured a desire for community in alternative churches, such as the Unitarian movement and, later, the Unitarian Universalist Association. The story of Black Unitarianism is typically told beginning with two key cities—New York City and Chicago—and small groups that rejected the idea of God but valued the ritualization of life and the forms of gathering offered by a humanistic church. In New York, after some years in ministry in Jamaica, Egbert Ethelred Brown (1914–1956), the first Black person ordained a Unitarian minister (1920), struggled but had little success advancing godless religion within Harlem. In reflecting on his ministry, Brown stated that he attended Meadville Theological School and became a Unitarian minister because "I decided that I was not compelled to be a minister of religion at all; but if I did enter the ministry I was under moral and spiritual compulsion to be a minister only of that church in which I could be absolutely honest."[1] First the Harlem Community Church, it became the Hubert Harrison Memorial Church (the name suggesting the theological and philosophical leanings of the congregation) and, in 1937, was finally named the Harlem Unitarian Church. Brown writes:

> The work of the Harlem Unitarian Church has been that of a great venture, admittedly undertaken without experience and without careful survey of local conditions, and without knowledge of the difficulties of the situation. This may be recorded now, as it ought to be, but it should be noted

that the necessity of this survey and knowledge were not recognized then. As far as I am concerned the fact is, that I sailed from the Island of Jamaica determined to establish a Unitarian Church in Harlem, and all that mattered to me in March 1920 was that the venture should be launched without delay. And it was.[2]

A staunch believer in a religion premised on freethought and critical engagement, Brown extended this commitment to various forms of community work. As opposed to consideration of traditional sacred texts such as the Bible, books about history, philosophy, and culture shaped conversation. Church services and gatherings hosted by Brown involved rigorous discussion and debate on important issues as a form of religious engagement that fed the mind. "In fact," according to Brown,

as far as the form of the meetings was concerned, they were not different from the services of other churches—hymns, prayers, Scripture readings and a sermon. But it was not long before we became impatient by reason of the slow growth in membership and of the unsatisfactory attendances. This impatience led to a radical change. We became what was called a Forum Church—more poetically,—a Temple and a Forum—; that is, everything continued as it was formerly, except that every sermon was followed by a free and full discussion from the floor . . . Its meetings were favorably referred to because the varied topics were interesting and challenging, and the speakers, colored and white, were very good.[3]

This was church, but, unlike other churches in Harlem, it wasn't the Christ-centered theology and faith one might gather from more prominent, mainline denominations that dominated Harlem's streets.

Brown struggled and was never able to secure a full and energetic endorsement from the Unitarian leadership. Despite doctrinal commitment to equality, Unitarianism in practice maintained a segregationist ethos, and so there was little— and always uneven—support for Brown's effort to expand the reach of Unitarianism into the Black community. His communication with Unitarian leadership demonstrated their limited interest in reaching the audience he intended. For them, an interracial church was a noble idea, but nothing they would actually work to achieve. This disappointed Brown, in light of what he saw as an ever-increasing potential audience, and a comparable need to move Black Americans away from superstition and toward reason and critical thinking. Such a repositioning would only serve to enhance their ability to gain traction in a world that had long denied them, and that they had shunned through a turn to heaven.

As other nontraditional forms of religiosity gained attention, Brown's efforts would eventually fade. But, under the leadership of Meadville Theological School graduate Lewis Allen McGee (1893–1979), efforts in Chicago were a bit more successful, while never reaching the growth and presence desired. And so, with Chicago, at least, as an example, Unitarianism offered Black Americans a place of ritual practice and performance of religious commitment without claims of transhistorical communications fueling worship. There was singing and centering moments, but no prayers to god(s); instead, there was reflection on human circumstances using the tools of human inquiry and speculation. Like Harlem with Brown, sermons (if they can be called such) in Chicago with McGee weren't about a special knowledge needed to secure eternal salvation and the end of death. They reflected on the here and now, on what takes place within the context of human history. Blacks within Unitarian communities restricted their claims to what could be verified, and this was the practice during the week and the content of fellowship on the weekend.

It wasn't until the civil rights movement, and the Black Power efforts in particular, that Unitarians—now the Unitarian Universalist Association (UUA)—were forced to take seriously and respond to racism within their ranks. Resources that had long been denied Black Unitarians were made available to address internal shortcomings. Figures like Reverend Mark Morrison-Reed rewrote the history of Unitarian Universalism so as to highlight the long-standing involvement of Black Americans. Godless worship was also rethought. Songs, styles of worship, and other ritual practices so often associated with Black churches were brought into the UUA as it sought to reflect a new sense of inclusion. Consequently, Blacks in the UUA have made the organization their own in numerous ways, including the development of infrastructure meant to help the UUA better practice diversity, equity, and inclusion as part of its self-understanding, and within all dimensions of its life and work. The UUA claims a theological orientation, but it is open and flexible, with the basic criteria involving the forging of meaning that enhances personal and collective life. Some members are theists, but many more seem nontheistic in their theological insights. While such a disparity wouldn't work within traditional Black churches, it isn't a significant challenge for the UUA, as individual congregations determine their general theological orientation. Over the past few years, in light of BLM, the UUA within many of its various dimensions has concerned itself with amplifying justice work in ways that reflect how it worships and how it spends its money. The question of Blackness, therefore, is much more prominent and the status and comfort of Black members of much greater concern. One of the significant examples of this shift is Black

Lives of Unitarian Universalism (BLUU), which is sponsored by the UUA. BLUU was founded in 2015 by Black Unitarian Universalists who attended the Movement for Black Lives gathering in Cleveland, Ohio. From that point on, the goal has been to foster a faith-fueled commitment within the UUA to "life-giving and life-saving opportunities for spiritual community and Black-centered organizing." Connected to the mission of BLM, BLUU understands itself and its objectives this way:

> Our hope is that this direct connection between our faith and the fight for Black liberation will make clear the urgent need for all those who call themselves Unitarian Universalists to declare, without caveat or clarification, that Black Lives Matter.[4]

In addition, we can see Black American involvement in the Ethical Culture movement, or what some reference as the Society for Ethical Culture. Founded in New York City through the efforts of Columbia University professor Felix Adler (1851–1933), Ethical Culture is a church-like organization that values fellowship and possesses a sense of wonder and awe—all grounded in the workings of the world with no theological attention to notions of the divine or transhistorical potentialities. Its aims, consistent with Adler's intent, are to forge increasingly productive modes of moral vision and worthwhile activity that advance the well-being of all life; in this way, it seeks to create a sense of life-meaning through an ethical commitment to producing "the good." Ethical Culture has struggled in terms of membership and is currently composed of roughly thirty congregations in total. But for some Black Americans it has represented an alternate source of community—the ability to gather on a Sunday, or for activities during the week, and to nurture one's mind through attention to pressing issues and to foster an earthy sense of justice and moral obligation.

Ethical Culture services, as are also the case with many Unitarian Universalist congregations, resemble what one would find at a typical Black Baptist or Methodist church any given Sunday. There is singing, often traditional hymns are altered to reflect nontheistic sensibilities and new ones created for this purpose. There are readings, opportunities for fellowship and sharing, and a sermon or lecture (the actual language can shift depending on the designated speaker). But, typically, there is no talk of God—and, certainly, the need for it isn't assumed.

AMERICAN HUMANIST ASSOCIATION

For some Black humanists, the churchiness of the UUA and Ethical Culture are too reminiscent of what they meant to leave behind, and for others it was a style of gathering they'd never found attractive. For these Black humanists, their meaning-making takes place within the context of organizations such as the American Humanist Association (AHA). Arguably the largest humanist organization in the country, with some ten thousand members, the AHA concerns itself with advancing a humanist agenda expressed through social change, and this appeals to Black humanists whose beliefs require personal involvement in transforming their social world. Moreover, it is explicitly opposed to supernatural claims, which would correspond to the antitheological stance of many Black humanists, and its commitment to separation of church and state parallels the motivations of some Black humanists who contest the unreasonable infringement of Black churches into the political arena. Furthermore, the AHA's devotion to the advancement of knowledge would satisfy the intellectual hunger of Black and white humanists alike, who see themselves as highly critical and well informed. Finally (although the list goes well beyond the dimensions named here), the presence of like-minded thinkers and the absence of the need to explain or justify one's nontheistic philosophy of life provides an opportunity to concentrate on the construction of a healthy existence. Nevertheless, issues related to social codes such as race remain and have to be addressed; these are places in the social mapping of life where the AHA has been behind the curve. Mindful of this, its leadership in the 2000s expressed a desire to improve by making substantive changes to its organizational structure (including the makeup of its governing board), goals, and related objectives. The intent of this work has been to decenter whiteness as the guiding logic. In other words,

> pursuing justice, equity, diversity and inclusion is a moral imperative for the American Humanist Association (AHA), and integral to our work as advocates. Humanist values require the affirmation of the inherent dignity of every human being, as well as the related need to create a society where all can flourish and become one's best self. We must dismantle systems of white supremacy and as humanists make it known that one of our most significant organizational goals is to fight for the rights of all marginalized communities. We acknowledge that many of our organizational founders and leaders, past and present, perpetuate and benefit from current systems of oppression. While we may be seen as "progressive" in some areas, we take responsibility for often being on the wrong side of justice. That history cannot be unlived, but facing these difficult truths allows us to do our best work going forward.[5]

Few, I would argue, understand what the AHA offers as being comparable to traditional modalities of theistic religion—but is the distinction that strong, outside of the preferred grammar and vocabulary of involvement? The AHA is concerned with fostering life-meaning, and it certainly serves as a mechanism for meaning-making in ways that wrestle with the fundamental questions of human existence. It ritualizes this quest through its annual conference and other regularized gatherings (e.g., lectures providing cautionary tales, celebration of achievements, and suggestions on living in right relationship). There is even what one might call the priesthood of central figures. Humanists such as historian of freethought Susan Jacoby might even be considered—to borrow language—prophets of an antitheological sort, who offer warnings and visionary pronouncements concerning the state of humanism as well as mechanisms for its advancement. If we observe carefully, we see also reverence for such figures, esteem for their writings, and, on occasion, quotation of their wise words in ways reminiscent of the regard bestowed upon the leadership of more traditional modalities of religiosity. No hymns are sung, but musical events, comedy, and other performances demonstrate a shared humanist ethos. The involvement of Black humanists in the AHA suggests a particular type of adherence to a religious form, not because the AHA is like traditional churches, but because its function is to foster life-meaning. We need only attend one of its conferences to garner a sense of community—of a group of the congenial that is evangelical in its commitment to advancing its nonbelief. I don't want to push this comparison too far, but to put it simply, the AHA does for many humanists (Black and non-Black) what Christian churches do for many theists (Black and non-Black).

BLACK NONBELIEVERS

A conversation with any group of Black humanists will eventually turn to the need to be with people who look like them and have experienced life in similar ways—people who get what it means to be Black. While this can be the case for Black humanists across the country, it can be particularly challenging for those living in the South, the Bible Belt. Dominique Huff makes this clear when discussing the Deep South, and the consequent importance of community. "The impetus for starting the group [a Facebook group for Black atheists]," Huff writes, "was made clear in a posting that read: 'given how obsessed people in Mississippi are with Christianity, being an atheist here is very isolating and difficult. Add to that the fact that I'm Black and nonheterosexual, and we're talking social suicide.'"[6] Put another way, existence outside Black theistic environments can place "black atheists in the no man's land between the black community they grew up in and the predominantly white world of atheists, agnostics and nonbelievers."[7] At the extreme, "in the black community, those who deny the existence of God are viewed as devil-possessed or deranged."[8] Mandisa Thomas recognizes the importance of online community as a space for Black humanists when she says,

> Many people felt as though they were helped in the transition out of their faith and to be able to find a community. With campaigns on social media and elsewhere, the messages that are shared can be a few words and even a couple paragraphs in order to share their story. This sharing of personal narratives can help bridge the gap of aloneness for many nonbelievers and help bring them together with fellow atheists and nonbelievers.[9]

The virtual community offered through Facebook groups and elsewhere has been useful for many Black humanists in that it constitutes a space free from judgment and condemnation, but for others physical gathering is desired. As one reporter notes, "Unlike other parts of the South where activities by black atheists remain online, Atlanta appears to be spearheading the momentum with the creation of nonbeliever organizations . . . which allow a previously marginalized minority a voice and a community that goes beyond anonymous avatars."[10] Black humanist communities, like more easily identified religious groupings, offer opportunities for self-formation, and for the ritualization of important life moments and challenges. There is a feeling that one is involved in something greater than oneself—not in a metaphysical sense, but, rather, because the communal is bigger and grander than the individual; it can't be defined simply as the sum of its parts.

The first decades of the twenty-first century have witnessed an increase in the number of communities created by and for Black humanists. In a context in which being Black can be a death sentence, and to be a Black nonbeliever is to multiply opportunities for ostracism, Black humanists need shelter. Candace Gorham has done a masterful job of pointing out the need for emotional and psychological assistance during troubled times. The effort of many humanists to address issues of loss or pain through reason falls flat, and they are not alone, as Gorham points out. Take the death of a loved one as an example:

> The problem is that grief blinds the mourner with dark, heavy clouds of blackness and blankets them in weighted shrouds of nothingness. Sometimes they need others to see for them. Sometimes they need others to feel for them. Sometimes they need others to think for them. Sometimes they just need others. And that is why the grief support industry thrives. What is lacking from that industry, however, is support for grieving nontheists. Nontheists are starved for support of a nonreligious or nonspiritual nature. They are looking for practical advice, just like everyone else, but they also need a special kind of support that makes room for their own particular existential struggle.[11]

Gorham calls for engagement that uses humanism to attend to the full range of human need. One such effort to meet these needs is the nonprofit Atlanta-based Black Nonbelievers (BN), organized and led by Mandisa Thomas. The aim of BN is clear: it "provides an informative, caring, festive and friendly community, and connects with other Blacks (and allies) who are living free of religion and might otherwise be shunned by family and friends. Instead of accepting dogma, we believe truth and morality are determined through reason and evidence."[12] There are some, as Thomas notes, who fail to recognize the need for a separate organization for Black humanists:

> You know, what's interesting is that we're still getting the question of, "Why does there have to be a Black Nonbelievers?" We have people who are protesting, who object to the Black Lives Matter movement and they object to the racial justice component of the secular community. I just find it very interesting because, with the advent of many well-known atheists and their behavior in the movement, it's high time that women and people of color—those whose voices have been obscured for a while—that our voices are heard more. I think there's still some push-back there, but I just try to keep my focus where it belongs, which is our members and the people who need us, as well as those who are our colleagues and work with us and know and are aware of the racial aspect and want to help.[13]

Founded in 2011, BN is far from a regional community. It has members and supporters outside of Georgia, and it is growing in terms of international recognition and partnerships (e.g., American Atheists, American Humanist Association, Freedom from Religion Foundation, Ex-Muslims of North America, Recovering from Religion, Secular Student Alliance, Secular Coalition, Foundation Beyond Belief, Secular Woman, and Center for Free Inquiry). A vibrant network cutting across the country—from Charlotte, North Carolina, to Detroit, Michigan, to Portland, Oregon, and beyond—BN is far reaching online as well. It provides a home for Black humanists, many of whom have experienced theism-related trauma or have been abandoned by friends and family because of their disbelief. BN helps individuals manage this trauma not simply through activities and written resources but through informal conversation as well as its welcoming posture. Health and well-being are fundamental to its aims. A look at its Facebook presence makes evident the energetic gatherings, the smiles and hugs, suggesting the ways in which BN constitutes a community. It is a welcoming place for Black humanists in a decidedly anti-Black and disbelief-fearing country. There are also ways in which BN provides a more balanced engagement with other humanist organizations: by connecting people to various groups without the discomfort that can arise when one moves around humanist circles as a Black humanist without the introduction and "cushioning"

BN affords. The organization serves as an expansive umbrella for a network of engagement that seeks to address every dimension of human life, through attention to every component of who we are as embodied beings living in the material world.

BN is diverse as well, since not all Black humanists are the same. There are class differences, differences in terms of sexual orientation, and differences in backstory regarding a history with, or without, theism. All of this is to say that BN works to make itself a safe space for Black humanists across a spectrum of life circumstances and orientations. One need only express an interest in the organization, respect its rules and regulations, and then participate as one likes and is able. To facilitate this approach, each affiliated group "regularly arranges events, projects, and social activities for members and guests."[14] A concern with the forging of robust life-meaning isn't explicitly stated as such, but the activities and the goals for BN activities certainly suggest a concern with a life grounded in reason, marked by fruitful relationships, that affirms the value and importance of nonbelievers. And, so, the aim is to develop an infrastructure of engagement that allows for a full range of social needs to be met and, in this way, maintain and advance humanist beliefs and practices.

The "fellowship community" is easily identified through merchandise, which proudly proclaims its existence. From T-shirts to coffee cups, merchandise does not simply financially supports the efforts of this organization; through these materials BN announces its presence and importance and visually indicates comfort with a public display of humanism. While many Black humanists feel isolated and believe they are alone, this merchandise tells a different story: there are lots of Black humanists, and, in a word, they are Black, and they are humanists . . . deal with it! As Thomas says, "We want to say, 'Hey, if you thought you were the only one out there, there are more of us, and we are here for you . . . We do seek to normalize atheism and destigmatize it, and one of the ways to do that is to be out."[15] BN also provides opportunities for self-realization and growth through lectures and other activities, and it offers the chance to commune with the likeminded through social events, including an annual cruise. Intellectual growth is promoted through discussion of new books related to Black humanism. Often seen in terms of extended family, BN affords a sense of life connected to others and in relationship. As Alix Jules, president of Black Nonbelievers of Dallas (a BN affiliate), makes clear: "For me and other Black nonbelievers like me, it's about turning Humanism from something we read about in books, into something that we do together."[16] In significant ways, BN works to untangle the assumed connections between Black culture and theism, and it does so in a manner that recognizes the power of joy, of fun:

BNN is very dedicated to maintaining a festive and grounded environment. While we strongly advocate for, and participate in, educational and informative activities, we also stress the importance of having fun and creating a relaxed atmosphere amongst fellow nonbelievers. Many of us are responsible for not only our careers and families, but also ourselves, and so having this outlet where we can let loose and let our hair down while building a strong foundation for support is crucial.[17]

This approach points out a path for Black humanists, enabling them to gain a greater sense of wholeness and more ease in expressing their desire for life-meaning in the company of others.

THE RELIGIOUS QUALITIES OF COMMUNITY

I end where I started: by making a distinction between religion and theism. My use of the language of religion isn't meant to attempt a blurring of difference. Rather, it's an effort to capture the dimensions of human life that aren't fully named through reason and to which the Black humanist community responds. As Greg Epstein notes, one can be good without God. There is a great deal behind this ability to be good—all sorts of moral and ethical connotations that, as he suggests, aren't confined to theistic ways of being in the world.[18]

This turn to the language of religion doesn't diminish the self-understanding, work, and efforts of the BN, of any other

Black humanist organization, or of any particular individual Black humanist. I am not trying to slip them into the cloud of great theistic witnesses. I do not intend to harness them with a sense of spirituality, although some members might embrace various modalities of spirituality (i.e., sensitivity to and an embrace of the larger web of life that connects humans to something more powerful than anything humans can create). I am not dismissing the pain and trauma many have felt when part of traditional religious communities, by which I mean theistic communities. As Thomas rightly notes,

> we have heard this from preachers who say blacks would not have gotten anywhere without faith. And if you do not believe in God, you are ostracized, targeted by family and friends, accused of trying to be white. There is this idea that if you subscribe to atheism, you are betraying your race, you are betraying your culture, you are betraying your history as well.[19]

I recognize and honor that pain, having experienced some of it myself as I moved out of my life as an evangelical minister. I understand that moving from one set of beliefs to another comes with a range of challenges and struggles. This is particularly true for the Black humanist, who is part of a larger Black community that remains decidedly theistic. As BN makes clear through its partnership with My Choice, My

Power Counseling, it is important to recognize that "whether you are newly out of religion or have been nonreligious for some time, Religious Trauma Syndrome may be affecting you more than realized, and this is a great opportunity to begin your healing process in. a safe and communal space."[20]

There is something to be said for Darrel Ray's sense of the need for more humanist involvement in the ritualization of life moments, though one might argue with some of his points. Ray, a founder of the Secular Therapist Project, remarks:

> the best we can do as humanists . . . is to talk about that pain in rational terms with the people who are suffering. We have humanist celebrants, as we'll call them, but they're focused on doing weddings. It takes a lot more training to learn how to deal with grief and loss. I don't see celebrants working in hospice or in hospitals, for example. There are secular people who need pastoral care, but we abdicate it to clergy.[21]

Ray is right in terms of this pressing need but wrong with respect to the range of activities undertaken by celebrants like Mandisa Thomas, who sees her full array of humanist activities as part of her charge as a celebrant. But, more than individual figures, there is the general ethos of Black humanism that recognizes loss and addresses it through community, and that honors the joys of life through humanist festivities.

In this way, many Black humanists have found strength and comfort in the company of other Black humanists and thereby rely on the goodwill and fellowship of other humans making their way through the world. BN, in a sense, works to make this movement through the world a little less painful and a little less lonely, but it is only one example of a growing network of organizations and fellowships that celebrate Black humanism. Black nontheists across the nation are forging sources of connection and community in a world still dominated by theistic organizations suspicious of—if not hostile toward—them.

ACKNOWLEDGMENTS

Over the years, I've had opportunity to lecture on Black humanism. Many of the ideas presented here developed in those lectures and in conversation after various events. In particular, the American Humanist Association, numerous Unitarian Universalist Association congregations, the Institute for Philosophical Research (Hannover, Germany), and the University of Humanistic Studies (Utrecht, Netherlands) offered me space to think about the importance of Black humanism. I'm grateful for those events and the growth in my thinking they promoted. Yet nothing would have come of those ideas developed in conversation with members of my humanist community without Jesseca Salky, and Salky Literary Management, who represented the project and brought it to the attention of Beacon Press. I couldn't be happier to be working again with my wonderful editor at Beacon, Amy Caldwell, and the rest of the staff that took this project from manuscript to published book. Thank you!

Finally, I want to thank my family and friends for their encouragement, and time away from the computer. The book began before the end of COVID and, without the support of my "village," I'm not certain I would have maintained the energy and focus necessary to get this book finished. Much appreciated. Much love. Next time, the fish and chips are on me!

NOTES

INTRODUCTION

1. Alejandra Molina, "Black Skeptics Uplift Their Community Through Social Justice," AP News October 15, 2020, https://apnews.com /article/race-and-ethnicity-religion-atheism-christianity-ee18e89b6a40 aae6689eea2e5a967fc5.

2. Sikivu Hutchinson, "The Unbearable Whiteness of Secular Studies," *LAProgressive*, December 26, 2016, https://www.laprogressive.com /science-and-religion-2/black-secular-studies.

3. Asher_Jak, "Religious Journey of a Black Lesbian Atheist," Rest for Resistance, September 1, 2017, https://restforresistance.com/zine /religious-journey-of-a-black-lesbian-atheist.

4. Ken Granderson, "Entrepreneurship as a Black Humanist," American Diversity Report, December 10, 2021, https://americandiversityreport .com/entrepreneurship-as-a-black-humanist-by-ken-granderson.

5. Hutchinson, *Humanists in the Hood*, 13.

6. Asher_Jak, "Religious Journey of a Black Lesbian Atheist."

7. I tend not to use the label "religious humanism" to express what I have in mind, because that terminology is so typically tied to the Unitarian Universalist Association and Ethical Culture, and using this label for predominantly white organizations can obscure the very ideas I mean to highlight.

8. Gorham, *On Death, Dying, and Disbelief*, 26.

9. American Atheists National Convention, https://convention
.atheists.org/speakers/mandisa-thomas (accessed June 24, 2022). For
information on the Universal Life Church see https://www.ulc.org
/about (accessed June 24, 2022). On the site it is described as "a
non-denominational religious organization that brings together people
from all walks of life. We embrace individuals across the spiritual
spectrum; anyone who wants to join our body of faith is welcome to
do so. Further, the ULC is proud to open its doors to all people,
regardless of gender, sexual orientation, race, ethnicity, or any other
defining characteristic."

10. "Activism Matters: Mandisa Thomas, Black Nonbelievers,"
AHS+, August 20, 2021, https://ahsplus.blog/2021/08/02/activism
-matters-mandisa-thomas-black-nonbelievers.

CHAPTER 2: A BRIEF (RELIGIOUS) HISTORY OF BLACK HUMANISM

1. Ken Granderson, "Entrepreneurship as a Black Humanist," American Diversity Report, December 10, 2021, https://americandiversityreport
.com/entrepreneurship-as-a-black-humanist-by-ken-granderson.

2. Ellison, "Blues People," 257.

3. For examples of African American folktales, see Henry Louis
Gates Jr. and Maria Tatar, *The Annotated African American Folktales*
(New York: Liveright, 2017), and Zora Neale Hurston, *Every Tongue
Got to Confess: Negro Folktales from the Gulf States* (New York: Amistad,
2002).

4. Ellison, "An Extravagance of Laughter," 146.

5. Quoted in Cameron, *Black Freethinkers*, 37.

6. Quoted from Hubert H. Harrison, "On a Certain Conservatism
in Negroes," in Pinn, *By These Hands*, 165–66.

7. Cameron, *Black Freethinkers*, 91.

8. Walter Everette Hawkins, "Too Much Religion," in *Messenger*,
November 1917, 27; quoted in Cameron, *Black Freethinkers*, 91.

9. Zora Neale Hurston, "Religion," from *Dust Tracks on a Road*
(1942), as found in Pinn, *By These Hands*, 181.

10. Larsen, "Quicksand," in *Quicksand and Passing*, 130.

11. Wright, *Black Boy*, 123–24.

12. Baldwin, *Go Tell It on the Mountain*.

13. Baldwin, *The Fire Next Time*.

14. From Baldwin, *The Fire Next Time*, in Pinn, *By These Hands*, 230–31.

15. William R. Jones, "The Case for Black Humanism," in Jones and Bruce, *Black Theology II*, 222–23.

16. From Alice Walker, "The Only Reason You Want to Go to Heaven Is That You Have Been Driven Out of Your Mind," in Pinn, *By These Hands*, 297.

17. Coates, *Between the World and Me*, 115.

CHAPTER 3: THE EVOLUTION OF BLACK HUMANISM

1. Sikivu Hutchinson, "The Unbearable Whiteness of Secular Studies," *LAProgressive*, December 26, 2016, https://www.laprogressive.com/science-and-religion-2/black-secular-studies.

2. David Niose, "Why Oprah's Anti-Atheist Bias Hurts So Much," *Psychology Today*, October 15, 2013, https://www.psychologytoday.com/us/blog/our-humanity-naturally/201310/why-oprahs-anti-atheist-bias-hurts-so-much.

3. Michael W. Chapman, "Steve Harvey on Atheists: 'To Me, You're an Idiot,'" CNS News, January 6, 2015, https://www.cnsnews.com/blog/michael-w-chapman/steve-harvey-atheists-me-you-re-idiot.

4. "On Black Atheism: Jamila Bey," *The Root*, December 3, 2011, https://www.theroot.com/on-black-atheism-mark-d-hatcher-1790867180.

5. "On Black Atheism: Mark D. Hatcher," *The Root*, December 3, 2011, https://www.theroot.com/on-black-atheism-mark-d-hatcher-1790867180.

6. "On Black Atheism: Mark D. Hatcher."

7. "On Black Atheism: Mark D. Hatcher."

8. Alejandra Molina, "Black Skeptics Uplift Their Community Through Social Justice," AP News, October 15, 2020, https://apnews.com/article/race-and-ethnicity-religion-atheism-christianity-ee18e89b6a40aae6689eea2e5a967fc5.

9. Asher_Jak, "Religious Journey of a Black Lesbian Atheist," Rest for Resistance, September 1, 2017, https://restforresistance.com/zine/religious-journey-of-a-black-lesbian-atheist.

10. Emily Brennan, "The Unbelievers," *New York Times*, November 25, 2011, https://www.nytimes.com/2011/11/27/fashion/african-american -atheists.html.

11. "Please Stop Assuming All Blacks Are Christian," *The Root*, October 2, 2013, https://www.theroot.com/please-stop-assuming-all -blacks-are-christian-1790898329.

12. See Gregory A. Smith, "About Three-in-Ten U.S. Adults Are Now Religiously Unaffiliated," Pew Research Center, December 14, 2021, https://www.pewresearch.org/religion/2021/12/14/about-three -in-ten-u-s-adults-are-now-religiously-unaffiliated.

13. See "Blacks Who Are Unaffiliated (Religious 'Nones')," Religious Landscape Study, Pew Research Center, https://www.pewresearch.org /religion/religious-landscape-study/religious-tradition/unaffiliated -religious-nones/racial-and-ethnic-composition/black, accessed June 21, 2022.

14. See Kiana Cox, "Nine-in-Ten Black 'Nones' Believe in God, but Fewer Pray or Attend Services," Pew Research Center, March 17, 2021, https://www.pewresearch.org/fact-tank/2021/03/17/nine-in-ten-black -nones-believe-in-god-but-fewer-pray-or-attend-services.

15. See Ryan P. Burge, "Black Americans See the Biggest Shift Away from Faith," *Christianity Today*, February 15, 2022, https://www .christianitytoday.com/news/2022/february/black-american-nones-faith -unaffiliation-nothing.html.

16. Burge, "Black Americans See the Biggest Shift Away from Faith."

17. Candace Gorham, Sikivu Hutchinson, Liz Ross, Bridgett Crutchfield, and Mandisa Thomas, "Five Fierce Humanists: Unapologetically Black Women Beyond Belief," *The Humanist*, June 19, 2018, https://thehumanist.com/magazine/july-august-2018/features/five-fierce -humanists-unapologetically-black-women-beyond-belief.

18. Kimberly Winston, "For Atheists of Color, 'Coming Out' Can Be Painful," *Washington Post*, February 23, 2012, https://www.washington post.com/national/on-faith/for-atheists-of-color-coming-out-can-be -painful/2012/02/23/gIQAVXqHWR_story.html.

19. Mandisa Thomas, "Confessions of a Black Atheist," CNN, March 28, 2015, https://www.cnn.com/2015/03/28/living/black-atheist -confession/index.html.

20. Danielle Butler, "Dating While Black and Atheist," *The Root*, October 11, 2017, https://www.theroot.com/dating-while-black-and -atheist-1819260656.

21. Molina, "Black Skeptics Uplift Their Community Through Social Justice."

22. Molina, "Black Skeptics Uplift Their Community Through Social Justice."

23. "Leaving the Black Church," *New Humanist*, June 23, 2020, https://newhumanist.org.uk/articles/5641/leaving-the-black-church.

24. Asher_Jak, "Religious Journey of a Black Lesbian Atheist."

25. Gorham, Hutchinson, Ross, Crutchfield, and Thomas, "Five Fierce Humanists."

CHAPTER 4: BLACK HUMANISM AND JUSTICE WORK

1. Christopher Cameron, "The New Black Atheists," Black Perspectives, December 3, 2016, https://www.aaihs.org/the-new-black-atheists.

2. Frederick Douglass, "An Unpublished Frederick Douglass Letter," in Pinn, *By These Hands*, 77.

3. Quoted in Van Deburg's commentary on Douglass's letter found at the end of Frederick Douglass, "An Unpublished Frederick Douglass Letter," in Pinn, *By These Hands*, 79.

4. See, for example, W. E. B. Du Bois, "A Soliloquy on Viewing My Life from the Last Decade of Its First Century," in *The Autobiography of W. E. B. Du Bois*, reprinted in Pinn, *By These Hands*, 216.

5. Huey P. Newton, "On the Relevance of the Church," reprinted in Pinn, *By These Hands*, 303.

6. Newton, "On the Relevance of the Church," 303.

7. Newton, "On the Relevance of the Church," 306.

8. Secured from "The Black Panther Party," African American Heritage, National Archives, https://www.archives.gov/research/african -americans/black-power/black-panthers, accessed June 23, 2022.

9. Quoted in Cameron, *Black Freethinkers*, 126.

10. "Black Manifesto," *New York Review of Books*, July 10, 1969, https://www.nybooks.com/articles/1969/07/10/black-manifesto, accessed June 23, 2022.

11. Chris Stedman, "Too Many Atheists Are Veering Dangerously Toward the Alt-Right," *Vice*, April 2, 2018, https://www.vice.com/en/article/3k7jx8/too-many-atheists-are-veering-dangerously-toward-the-alt-right.

12. Sincere Kirabo, "What Sam Harris Gets Wrong About Racism and Violence in America," *HuffPost*, August 24, 2016, https://www.huffpost.com/entry/what-sam-harris-gets-wron_b_11680182.

13. Kirabo, "What Sam Harris Gets Wrong About Racism and Violence in America."

14. Sikivu Hutchinson, "Black Secular Teen Activists: Unchurched and 'Un-bossed,'" *HuffPost*, December 26, 2017, https://www.huffpost.com/entry/black-secular-teen-activists-unchurched-and-un-bossed_b_5a427c4ee4b0dfode8b06706.

15. Hutchinson, "Black Secular Teen Activists."

16. President Barack Obama's Inaugural Address, January 21, 2009, https://obamawhitehouse.archives.gov/blog/2009/01/21/president-Barack-obamas-inaugural-address.

17. See "Herstory," Black Lives Matter, https://blacklivesmatter.com/herstory, accessed June 23, 2022.

18. Candace Gorham, Sikivu Hutchinson, Lizz Ross, Bridgett Crutchfield, and Mandisa Thomas, "Five Fierce Humanists: Unapologetically Black Women Beyond Belief," *The Humanist*, June 19, 2018, https://thehumanist.com/magazine/july-august-2018/features/five-fierce-humanists-unapologetically-black-women-beyond-belief.

19. "BLM Demands," Black Lives Matter, https://blacklivesmatter.com/blm-demands, accessed June 23, 2022.

20. Norm R. Allen Jr., "Humanism and the Black Lives Matter Movement," *Norm Allen's Reasonings*, June 12, 2019, https://www.kurtzinstitute.org/news-commentary?category=reasonings, accessed June 23, 2022.

21. Sincere Kirabo, "Humanism and the #BlackLivesMatter Movement," *The Humanist*, March 2, 2015, https://thehumanist.com/commentary/humanism-and-the-blacklivesmatter-movement.

22. The Black Humanist Alliance, "Humanism Goes Hand-in-Hand with Racial Justice and #BlackLivesMatter," *The Humanist*, May 10, 2016, https://thehumanist.com/news/aha_news/humanism-goes-hand-hand-racial-justice-blacklivesmatter.

23. Melynda Price, "The Sacred Secular Politics of Black Lives Matter," The Immanent Frame, September 22, 2016, https://tif.ssrc.org/2016/09/22/religion-secularism-and-black-lives-matter.

24. Hebah H. Farrag and Ann Gleig, "Far from Being Anti-Religious, Faith and Spirituality Run Deep in Black Lives Matter," *The Conversation*, September 14, 2020, https://theconversation.com/far-from-being-anti-religious-faith-and-spirituality-run-deep-in-black-lives-matter-145610.

25. Farrag and Gleig, "Far from Being Anti-Religious, Faith and Spirituality Run Deep in Black Lives Matter."

26. See "Herstory," Black Lives Matter.

CHAPTER 5: BLACK HUMANISTS IN COMMUNITY

1. Egbert Ethelred Brown, "A Brief History of the Harlem Unitarian Church," September 11, 1949, https://files.meadville.edu/files/resources/brief-history-of-harlem-unitarian-church.pdf, 3, accessed June 24, 2022.

2. Brown, "A Brief History of the Harlem Unitarian Church," 5.

3. Brown, "A Brief History of the Harlem Unitarian Church," 6–7.

4. See Black Lives of Unitarian Universalism, "Our Story," https://blacklivesuu.org/our-story/, and Unitarian Universalist Association, https://www.uua.org/giving/areas-support/funds/promise-and-practice/history-black-lives-uu, accessed June 24, 2022.

5. See American Humanist Association, "Statement on Justice, Equity, Diversity, and Inclusion," https://americanhumanist.org/key-issues/statements-and-resolutions/equity, accessed July 9, 2022.

6. Kim Chakanetsa, "Black, Atheist, and Living in the South," CNN, December 8, 2011, https://religion.blogs.cnn.com/2011/12/08/black-atheist-and-living-in-the-south.

7. Jeff Kunerth, "Black Atheists Search for Sense of Belonging," *Gainesville Sun*/Gainesville.com, April 3, 2013, https://www.gainesville.com/story/news/2013/04/04/black-atheists-search-for-sense-of-belonging/31845594007.

8. Kunerth, "Black Atheists Search for Sense of Belonging."

9. Scott Douglas Jacobsen, "#BNChangesLives and Lives Changed by Black Nonbelievers, Inc.," The Good Men Project, May 10, 2018, https://goodmenproject.com/uncategorized/bnchangeslives-and-life-sjbn, accessed June 24, 2022.

10. Chakanetsa, "Black, Atheist, and Living in the South."

11. Gorham, *On Death, Dying, and Disbelief*, 11.

12. See "Who We Are," Black Nonbelievers, https://blacknonbelievers.org/who-we-are, accessed June 24, 2022. For an interesting, and global, take on the importance of ritualization through ceremonies in line with what BNN seeks to offer, see Giovanni Gaetani, "The Importance of Humanist Ceremonies—and Why You Should Consider Introducing Them in Your Country," Humanists International, November 12, 2020, https://humanists.international/blog/the-importance-of-humanist-ceremonies-and-why-you-should-consider-introducing-them-in-your-country.

13. Andrew J. Rausch, "A Conversation with Mandisa Thomas, President of Black Nonbelievers, Inc.," *Secularbynature*, April 10, 2018, https://secularbynature.wordpress.com/2018/04/10/a-conversation-with-mandisa-thomas-president-of-black-nonbelievers-inc.

14. "Black Non-Believers," Northern Indiana Atheists, https://northernindianaatheists.com/education/2018/6/11/black-non-believers, accessed June 24, 2022.

15. Jessica Lipscomb, "Miami Atheists Demand to Be Heard," *Miami New Times*, December 18, 2018, https://www.miaminewtimes.com/news/miamis-atheist-community-and-organizations-are-growing-10955178.

16. Zachary Moore, "Interview: Alix Jules on Black Nonbelievers," Fellowship of Freethought, February 21, 2013, https://fofdallas.org /category/groups/black-nonbelievers.

17. Administrator, "An Introduction to Black Nonbelievers, Inc.," Go Humanity, February 22, 2013, https://gohumanity.world/an -introduction-to-black-nonbelievers-inc.

18. Epstein, *Good Without God*.

19. Kimberly Winston, "For Atheists of Color, 'Coming Out' Can Be Painful," *sojourners*, February 24, 2012, https://sojo.net/articles /atheists-color-coming-out-can-be-painful.

20. See "Religious Trauma Group Coaching," Black Nonbelievers, https://blacknonbelievers.org/religious-trauma-group-coaching, accessed June 24, 2022.

21. Samuel G. Freedman, "In a Crisis, Humanists Seem Absent," *New York Times*, December 28, 2012, https://www.nytimes.com/2012 /12/29/us/on-religion-where-are-the-humanists.html.

WORKS CITED

Alexander, Nathan G. *Race in a Godless World: Atheism, Race, and Civilization, 1850–1914.* New York: New York University Press, 2019.

Allen, Norm. *African American Humanism.* Amherst, NY: Prometheus, 1991.

———. *The Black Humanist Experience: An Alternative to Religion.* Amherst, NY: Prometheus, 2002.

Baldwin, James. *The First New Time.* New York: Vintage, 1992.

———. *Go Tell It on the Mountain.* New York: Knopf, 1953.

Barbera, Don. *Black and Not Baptist: Nonbelief and Freethought in the Black Community.* iUniverse, 2003.

Camara, Jeremiah. *Holy Lockdown: Does the Church Limit Black Progress?* Lilburn, GA: Twelfth House, 2004.

———. *The New Doubting Thomas: The Bible, Black Folks, and Blind Belief.* Lilburn, GA: Twelfth House, 2010.

Cameron, Christopher. *Black Freethinkers: A History of African American Secularism.* Evanston, IL: Northwestern University Press, 2019.

Coates, Ta-Nehisi, *Between the World and Me*. New York: Spiegel & Grau, 2015.

Ellison, Ralph. *Going to the Territory*. New York: Vintage International, 1995.

———. *Shadow and Act*. New York: Vintage International, 1995.

Epstein, Greg. *Good Without God: What a Billion Nonreligious People Do Believe*. New York: William Morrow, 2009.

People Do Believe. New York: William Morrow, 2009.

Evans, D. K. *Emancipation of a Black Atheist*. Durham, NC: Pitchstone, 2017.

Floyd-Thomas, Juan M. *The Origins of Black Humanism in America: Reverend Ethelred Brown and the Unitarian Church*. New York: Palgrave Macmillan, 2008.

Forman, James. *The Making of Black Revolutionaries*. Washington, DC: Open Hand, 1985.

Garst, Karen L. *Women Beyond Belief: Discovering Life Without Religion*. Durham, NC: Pitchstone, 2016.

Gorham, Candace R. M. *The Ebony Exodus Project: Why Some Black Women Are Walking Out on Religion—and Others Should Too*. Durham, NC: Pitchstone, 2013.

———. *On Death, Dying, and Disbelief*. Durham, NC: Pitchstone, 2021.

Hansberry, Lorraine. *A Raisin in the Sun*. New York: Vintage, 2004.

Harrison, Hubert H. *The Negro and the Nation*. New York: Cosmo-Advocate, 1917.

Hart, William David, ed. *Educating Humanists: The Challenge of Sustaining Communities in the Contemporary Era*. New York: Palgrave Macmillan, 2022.

Hurston, Zora Neale. *Dust Tracks on a Road*. New York: Harper-Collins, 1970.

Hutchinson, Sikivu. *Godless Americana: Race and Religious Rebels*. Los Angeles: Infidel, 2013.

————. *Humanists in the Hood: Unapologetically Black, Feminist, and Heretical*. Durham, NC: Pitchstone 2020.

————. *Moral Combat: Black Atheists, Gender Politics, and Values Wars*. Los Angeles: Infidel, 2011.

Jones, William R. *Is God a White Racist? A Preamble to Black Theology*. Boston: Beacon, 1996.

Jones, William R., and Calvin E. Bruce, eds. *Black Theology II*. Lewisburg, PA: Bucknell University Press, 1978.

Larsen, Nella. "Quicksand." In *Quicksand and Passing*, 1–135. New Brunswick, NJ: Rutgers University Press, 1986.

Mays, Benjamin. *The Negro's God: As Reflected in His Literature*. Eugene, OR: Wipf & Stock, 2010.

McGowan, Dale, and Anthony B. Pinn, eds. *Everyday Humanism*. London: Equinox, 2014.

Miller, Monica R., ed. *Humanism in a Non-Humanist World*. New York: Palgrave Macmillan, 2018.

Miller, R. Baxter. *Black American Literature and Humanism*. Lexington: University Press of Kentucky, 2021.

Morrison-Reed, Mark. *Black Pioneers in a White Denomination.* Boston: Skinner House, 1992.

———. *Darkening the Doorways: Black Trailblazers and Missed Opportunities in Unitarian Universalism.* Boston: Skinner House, 2011.

———. *In Between: Memoir of an Integration Baby.* Boston: Skinner House, 2008.

Newton, Huey P. *To Die for the People: The Writings of Huey P. Newton.* San Francisco: City Lights, 2009.

Pinn, Anthony B. *African American Humanist Principles: Living and Thinking Like the Children of Nimrod.* New York: Palgrave Macmillan, 2004.

———. *By These Hands: A Documentary History of African American Humanism.* New York: New York University Press, 2001.

———. *The End of God-Talk: An African American Humanist Theology.* New York: Oxford University Press, 2012.

———. *Humanism: Essays on Race, Religion, and Popular Culture.* London: Bloomsbury Academic, 2015.

———. *What Is Humanism, and Why Does It Matter?* New York: Routledge, 2016.

———. *When Colorblindness Isn't the Answer: Humanism and the Challenge of Race.* Durham, NC: Pitchstone, 2017.

———. *Writing God's Obituary: How a Good Methodist Became a Better Atheist.* Amherst, NY: Prometheus, 2014.

Pinn, Anthony B., ed. *Humanism and the Challenge of Difference.* New York: Palgrave Macmillan, 2018.

———. *The Oxford Handbook of Humanism*. New York: Oxford University Press, 2021.

Walker, Alice. *Anything We Love Can Be Saved: A Writer's Activism*. New York: Random House, 1997.

Walker, Alice. *The Color Purple*. New York: Harvest, 2003.

Wright, Richard. *Black Boy and American Hunger*. New York: Perennial Classics, 1998.

INDEX